Manifesto for Philosophy

SUNY series,
Intersections: Philosophy and Critical Theory
Rodolphe A. Gasché, Editor

MANIFESTO FOR PHILOSOPHY

BY ALAIN BADIOU

Followed by Two Essays:
"The (Re)turn of philosophy *itself*"
and
"Definition of philosophy"

Translated, edited, and with an introduction by
Norman Madarasz

State University of New York Press

Published by
State University of New York Press, Albany

For information, address State University of New York
Press, State University Plaza, Albany, N.Y., 12246

Production by Diane Ganeles
Marketing by Nancy Farrell

Library of Congress Cataloging-in-Publication Data

Badiou, Alain.
    [Manifeste pour la philosophie. English]
    Manifesto for philosophy : followed by two essays : "The
(re)turn of philosophy itself" and "Definition of philosophy / by
Alain Badiou ; translated, edited, and with an introduction by
Norman Madarasz.
        p.   cm. — (SUNY series, Intersections : philosophy and
critical theory)
    Includes bibliographical references and index.
    ISBN 0-7914-4219-5 (hc : alk. paper). —
ISBN 0-7914-4220-9 (pbk. : alk. paper)
    1. Philosophy. II. Badiou, Alain. Le (re)tour de la philosophie
elle-même. English. 1999. III. Title. IV. Series :
Intersections (Albany, N.Y.)
    B2430.B273M3713   1999
    101—dc21   98-43903
                                                        CIP

10 9 8 7 6 5 4 3 2 1

CONTENTS

INTRODUCTION:

The Event, or Launching Philosophical Intervention
— Openings onto Alain Badiou's philosophical system —

Hegel once wrote that Truth could not be expressed within a single sentence. His statement could surely be taken as justification for the length of his books. Then again, the very fact that he needed the apparatus of the sentence to state his own truth suggests that the expressive technique of the sentence is as tricky, indeed undecidable, as the question of Truth itself. Ultimately, the discerning-power of the sentence falls short of the speculative split required to treat concepts out of the evidence and certainty of Presence. Its inadequacy stems more perhaps from its relying on expression as a vehicle than from its elementary structure.

Our modern times have seen Truth relativized, allotted with value and distanced from the Absolute. Inversely, the very essence of the shifting points of view specific to relativity have been located in the sentence as much as in physical movement itself. Philosophy has certainly not been left unscathed by relativity, nor has it been a lone bystander. Nietzsche had in any case already anticipated it. By opening itself to relativity, philosophical thought has grown increasingly aware of its boundaries, its borders—and its frontiers. These frontiers are precisely the points whereby philosophy asks the question of the nature of Truth and the particular ways in which it can be thought, something best considered as a philosophical experience. These frontiers are also those at which we raise the query as to whether Truth actually proves to be a well-founded fiction, somewhat of a more sophistic experience. As the study of Truth in its presence, absence, or deferral is what philosophy generally recognizes as its singular aim and duty, how and what is to be transmitted of this Truth becomes a problem akin to the status of Truth itself. From silence to explosion, from lack to excess, from inner recesses to protuberant outskirts, there lies in philosophy the knotted intricacy of dualateral thinking. If Truth cannot be expressed in a single sentence, what means of its transmission is apt enough to mold it into the shape of speech or the written script? What language is needed to contain such a transmission? What mode places us on the same plane of inquiry as Truth devoid of substance, but imbued with thought?

To such questions regarding accessibility to Truth, Alain Badiou would add the following problems. First, the type of logic required to assure the thinkable consistency of our investigation. Second, the type of decision required regarding the ontology through which its concept-building will be made possible. Since at least 1963, in the very specific activity of mathematics known as set theory, the question of the logic needed to understand how a statement delivers its content and the type of vehicle it uses to send its idea has preoccupied practitioners in the field. What the mathematician Paul Cohen brought in that year with his theory of the 'undecidable' regarding the nature of a mathematical theorem, namely Georg Cantor's continuum problem, was the *proof* of a sentence being neither true nor false.[1]

The philosophical act begins with the springing forth of such an undecidable. This is an instance of what Alain Badiou calls an event, whose occurrence can be granted as being rare, haphazard and incalculable. The event should not be taken in the context of, say, Donald Davidson's theory of action, nor should it be considered as rare by the way it is designated or judged. If the event is rare, it is so by definition, i.e., it is a surging forth of non-being. Now, the statement as undecidable, initiated by Bertrand Russell's paradox and exemplified by Kurt Gödel's first theorem, is the kind of event which launches the notion of philosophical "intervention." Its discrimination does not rely on the computable force of arithmetic, nor on the diagrammatic compactness of geometry. Intervention seeks out that ever-proliferating grounding promise of mathematics: the multiple, the set. Philosophical intervention, in its attempts at maintaining the greatest fidelity to the nature of an event in its occurrence, must think through the immanent organization of uncountable multiplicities. For the event is the surging forth of what precisely cannot be counted, a subtraction of the One to the benefit of the pure multiple.

Alain Badiou is Professor of Philosophy at University of Paris 8, the former Vincennes University. He is part of the original staff appointed by Michel Foucault in 1969 at the then-experimental research center. He is also currently Conference Director at the Collège International de Philosophie in Paris. His education and training are in philosophy and mathematics. Apart from his work in philosophy, Professor Badiou is also an accomplished playwright.

Manifesto for Philosophy was published in 1989 as *Manifeste pour la philosophie*. Two additional essays have been included here, "The (Re)turn of Philosophy Itself" and "Definition of Philosophy," both of which appeared under the heading "Philosophy Itself" in *Conditions* (Paris: Seuil, 1992), an anthology of essays and conferences given at the turn of the decade. This is the first translation of one of his major works in English.

Points of entry into Badiou's thinking are many and not always homogenous, nor do they only gravitate around a central strategy. Ultimately the text itself will shed adequate light on this spectrum. Let it suffice for the purposes of these remarks to defend in the strictest sense of rationalism that Badiou's text is a work of thought which aims at drawing the link between intervening upon the site of an event and the fundamental void from which the event arises. For any statement on the event is ultimately one regarding the void. An event triggered by chance and confluence, coincidence and conjuncture, by definition begins something new. It complements and alters a situation by its incalculable surprise, disappearing as soon as it springs forth. Every philosophical act is the fruit of a decision about this event.

Both *Manifesto* and "The (Re)turn of Philosophy Itself" are densely developed presentations of the contemporary philosophical context in which Professor Badiou's major work *L'Etre et l'événement* was published in 1988. In the thirty–seven 'Meditations' of that opus, he undertook the grounding of philosophy from a compendium of 'conceptual personae' (to use an expression he frequently enjoys borrowing from the late Gilles Deleuze). From 'Plato/Cantor' to 'Descartes/Lacan', this compendium was strung together with the axioms of set theory. The conceptual personae, and the way they are assembled, merely emphasize a rejection of historicism in philosophy. The greatest thinkers of the West are placed on a common plane, whose rhythm is punctuated by the progression of the idea of pure multiplicity. Badiou's aim was to twist the historic narrative of philosophy's development, in versions as varied as the academic treatment of organizing philosophy to Heidegger's vision of interpreting it as a history of (the forgetting of) Being, so as to instead follow the unfolding of the mathematical dimension, whose structure he identifies as being that of ontology's.

By steering away from historicism, Badiou argues against the notion of the end of philosophy. In so doing, he sees its current critical state, at least in France, as the reflection of a general social malaise provoked by a rupturing of the sacred ties that used to bind our social lives together. The end of philosophy traces social alienation instead of a depletion of its own capacities. Philosophy must recognize the disorientation of our epoch as the cloth on which its patterns spread and assemble. It must carve out the disorientation and integrate it immanently into its operation. If philosophy has any chance of escaping from historicism, and thus from the obsessive fetishization of its finitude or end, a temporal arc of simultaneity must join the different moments of thought together.[2] A key ingredient to this vision of organizing thought is the argument that ontology is actually mathematics, i.e., Being as pure multiple in its infinite proliferation is what mathematics *says*: "that mathematics, in all of its historic becoming, pronounces what is utterable of being *qua* being."[3]

In a recent survey of philosophy in France since the 1970s, Dominique Janicaud sets the record straight when emphasizing that *L'Etre et l'événement*, "is the first book since *Being and Time* which again dares to ask the question of 'What about being *qua* being?', and brings forth an answer to it . . ."[4] While Badiou does not quite cite Aristotle in saying that being can be said in many ways, his use of Aristotelian terminology belies the fact that his being is an unbounded idea of multiplicity. His ontology is one of the pure multiple, a multiple that cannot be "counted as one," a multiple in term-to-term relation with the basic notion of a multiple or set in Set Theory (here using the Zermelo-Fraenkel version). The paradoxes and undecidables of that theoretical attempt to found mathematical reasoning are also those of ontology.

Set Theory also consists of an approach at understanding the foundations of reasoning in general. Its origins stem from number theory, in which Peano provided the first axiomatization of addition, thereby explaining the inductive steps made in moving from one number to another in the series of natural numbers. Badiou's axiomatization of ontology deals with the traditional categories of metaphysics. It also attempts to integrate the category of being—and here may we find the divergence in his application of Set Theory to knowledge in general. As concerns the field of logic, the subtractive nature of being, and the radical nature of the event or non-being, had disappeared ever since being excluded—or debarred—by C.S. Peirce. What does this give when Badiou brings axiomatization to human experience? Something akin to the descriptions in Samuel Beckett's later work. In one of his most elegant essays, Badiou portrays Beckett's text as pointing to a stylistic economy seen as "ancient, or categorical. . . . What is woven in the course of [his post-1960 work] are the five supreme genera of Plato's *Sophist*. These genera are the latent concepts for seizing humanity's generic existence. They underscore prosodic destitution as that from which a thinking of our destiny is made possible. The supreme genera of Movement, Rest, the Same, the Other and Logos are the shifted variants of the Platonic proposition, constituting the earmarks, or primitive terms, of an axiomatic distribution of humanity as such."[5] This is indeed, to cite the title of a work of Nelson Goodman's, a way of world-making.

From the perspective of logic, Badiou's entire embracing of set theory seeks to correct two fundamental philosophical mistakes. The first involves a clearer understanding and renewal of the traditional concepts populating our metaphysics. The second takes on the 'onto-theological' misrepresentation of the infinite within philosophy, a need to secularize the infinite so as to leave the bind of humanity's finitude—something mathematicians have done for well over a century.

Badiou develops what he terms a "meta-ontology". In so doing, he pleads for a stratification of discourses. This meta-ontology aims to make use of mathematical fragments which, from its own field, would allow philosophy the ability to articulate two discourses and practices different from it. The first such discourse is mathematics, i.e., the science of being. The second involves the intervening doctrines of the event, i.e., those designating that-which-is-not-being-*qua*-being. Its hypothetical departure point is that every 'object' is reducible to a pure multiplicity, itself edified upon naming the void in the Axiom of the Empty Set.[6]

There does, however, exist the problem of mathematicians' assent with this hypothesis. Badiou feels it is possible to accept that within the field of the working mathematician, these choice fragments of mathematics, namely the objects of Set theory, can remain inactive as theoretical apparatuses. While within meta-ontology, they are required and singular underpinnings. An essential theorem of his system is that Truth makes a hole in sense, i.e., Truth is not given to presence, not to mention representation. Truth has no object. "It is of the essence of ontology to be executed in the reflexive debarring of its identity."[7] Which means that in the emergence of the subjective pragmatics of this Truth-operation, ontology, or mathematics, remains in a disobjectivated or split relation to its identity. As Badiou emphasizes, mathematics could easily do without philosophical speculation about its field owing to philosophy's interest in the sense of its discourse and its reference. Being has no sense. Nor does the Truth by which it is transmitted

in a subjective process. Nor, consequently, does
Badiou's approach aim at labeling sense onto mathematical discourse.

In short, Badiou embarks upon a renewed
attempt at grounding philosophy, laid out in a vision
at once controversial and antipathetic to many contemporary thinkers, especially in France. However,
could such an alternative have been overlooked any
longer as the streets and airwaves of continental
Europe harkened to the clarion call of the End of philosophy, or folded under attempts to return to neo-
Kantianism? These days, there is an end to everything.
The youthful rabble-rousing virtuosity of yesteryear of
breaking with tradition now seems in hindsight the
evacuation grounds of the constructs which link
thought to an evolving world. If philosophy is in any
way nearing an 'end', the knowledge of what it is that
is ending, or not, is the logical step to try in order to
move forward. It is also the one this French philosopher embarks on.

To achieve this move away from the claim of philosophy's ending, Badiou proceeds by examining the
nature of the philosophical act. The event is the throw
of the dice beginning a process borne in what can be
considered as one of the conditions of philosophy.[8] In
the Socratic Dialogues, Plato originated the idea that
philosophy coexists in the neighborhood of other
types of creative knowledge. Dialectics interrupted the
cosmogony of Greek mythology in the *Republic*. The
structure of its *mise-en-scène*, the medium used to
express it, namely the poem, and to a lesser extent
art, were held as an alternative, however misleading if
not threatening, to dialectics. Also in the *Republic*, the
demonstration of justice had to rely upon the analogi-
cal power and constructive dictates of the political.
Further still, the skill of geometry allowed mere slaves

to enter into the wisdom of the highest of worlds, as in the *Meno*. And Socrates' restless wandering would have stumbled onto distraught hearts had love not been a motivating force in his devotion to wisdom as well as in the care with which he embraced his young disciples, as can be read by all in the *Symposium* and *Pheadrus*.

Art, science, the political and love: these are the conditions of philosophy as traced in Plato's thinking. These are the domains in which the event may arise, seeking its discrimination through them and determination in a gesture of careful naming. They are procedures that in their immanence are capable of truth. The expression of this truth in its completion follows what Badiou sees as a perpetually deferred process within the field of a given procedure. In no way is it linked to producing Truth itself. The truth of the being of an event, faithful to its evanescence, will only have been uttered in some future time of discerning, which no sentence can reach in its completed form.

All of this once the dice fall. The motif is from the French nineteenth-century poet Stéphane Mallarmé, as is the method of 'Restrictive Action' (*action restreinte*) in light of his unfinished Book, which Badiou transposes onto philosophy. This is the very meaning of his effort of intervening on the site of an event. Not to represent or reproduce the event, but to capture the truths it bears through a given condition and to ultimately seize the truth of its being. Just as Mallarmé spoke of an egalitarian strategy of writing, devoid of Presence, provoked by an event, with the crowd as the ultimate destination of the poem, so also does Badiou, by shifting and sliding the notion over to philosophical action.

Philosophy is in the age of its disorientation. Threatened by dissolution into the poem, journalism, science and ethics, philosophy can be said to be "sutured" to its own conditions and other fields. In an interview given to *Les Temps Modernes* in 1990, Badiou explained that the suture is the very mode of linking-up that Heidegger "proposed between philosophy on the one hand and the poem on the other. . . . What continues to be a valid question is to know whether philosophy can truly be summoned to the poetic statement as if, in the historical destiny of thought in our time, it were the only resource and the only recourse of a turnabout toward being."[9] At its worst fate, i.e., as a museum figure, philosophy sees itself dissolved into its representation as completed and over. Hence a current specter: doing philosophy can often be accompanied by the excitement of a visit meant to honor an embalmed deceased demon.

Badiou is convinced of quite the opposite. He defines restrictive action in philosophy as postulating no single form of general orientation. He takes it as an endeavor to place this thinking of disorientation under the rule of points of orientation in order to once again find a régime of the *immanent* rules of philosophy. This action involves "desuturing" philosophy from the fragmentation of disoriented thought. Desuturing releases philosophy from its recent tendency of relying on the conditions (i.e., the matheme, poem, the political and love) to highlight the fact of having misguidedly taken a truth as being its own. If it has at any time been legitimate to speak of Truth in terms of a fiction, its sources can be found as caused by such acts of suture. The philosophical thinking exposed in the system of the *Manifesto* attests to a torsion in which language is shattered so as to be dislodged from the dominance of sense, while Truth is distinguished from the truths produced by the conditions of philosophy. Philosophy produces no truths.

Step by step then, the nature of philosophical 'intervention' consists in capturing what is the closest to the event itself, the very truth behind its eventful status, i.e., being multiple. "I call intervention every procedure by which a multiple is recognized as an event."[10] More so, the inscription of such recognition arises from an act of naming. Without an event there would be no truth in a situation, only what Badiou terms "veridicality". An event supplements a situation wherein the four conditions are found to coexist. Consequently, an attempt at naming the event must also be a supplement, an addition, indeed a supernumenary intervention.

Badiou names the kind of truth most faithful to the being of an event: Generic truth. The act of naming is testimony to the fact that philosophy painstakingly approaches truths, i.e., linked to events arising within each of the conditions or Generic procedures, as only mis-said or half said. This is an integral inscription of the fact that an attempt at reeling truths into Presence, in claiming possibilities of full head-on illumination, must take account of the event in its evanescent fleeing into nondescript shadows. "Is it possible to *name* that which happens or befalls in terms of it befalling?" asks Badiou.[11] In other words, that which we can ascertain as not presented must at least offer a proper name to presentation.[12] Naming is thus an act or rather an attempt at capturing the pure multiple in the trace of the written word. As Mallarmé writes, "Your act always applies to paper; for meditating, traceless, grows evanescent, nor is instinct exalted in some vehement and lost gesture, which you sought."[13]

What this act of naming involves is outlined in Badiou's "theory of canonical names". This theory is meant to refute Leibniz's claim that within a given situation, S, an indiscernible, if it exists, can only be known by God, i.e., from a point of overall transcendence. According to Leibniz, no indiscernible is within the rational grasp of an agent in situation S. No two things on Earth can be said to be exactly identical.

The demonstration is developed according to the following guiding principles. Let S designate the fundamental situation that a group of agents can call *their* world. In a given extension of a fundamental situation, S, the extension is generic, S(♀), if and only if it is connected, as it were, to S. The generic element of this extension comprises the existence of an indiscernible. The theory of canonical names stipulates that for a given name in S, the existence of an indiscernible in S(♀) can be proved by situating the referential value of a name in '♀'. That 'value' is such that the only reference given to the name, α, in S(♀), is another name, μ, in S. 'μ' is a name in S if it defines the ordered pair, $\mu_n = <\mu(n), \pi>$, where μ is distributed in a hierarchical ordinal, n, and π is the minimal set of conditions. As Badiou writes, "the 'nominalist' singularity of the generic extension, S(♀), is such that its elements are only accessible by their names."[14] What is more is that we are faced with a situation where a name makes the thing. The name cannot mean just anything, as the generic extension, S(♀), is forced, as it were, to remain linked to the fundamental or basic situation, S, and μ is determined to be the ♀-referent of a name of S. Such connectedness confirms the Lacanian precept that "there is no metalanguage" for there is never complete separation from language's powers of immersion. Following this argument, there can be no position akin to that of God's eye.

The interested reader should consult Meditation 34 of *L'Etre et l'événement* for the complete demonstration. Let us just briefly summarize Badiou's results regarding an enlarged S in which there exists a generic procedure.

— $S \subset S(♀)$. Hence $S(♀)$ is an extension.

— $♀ \in S(♀)$. $S(♀)$ is a proper extension, as $\neg(♀ \in S)$

Owing to this last stipulation, it can be seen that there is no supplementary ordinal in $S(♀)$. The natural ingredient of the indiscernible is the ordinal, whereas the referent of the artificial part is the intra-ontological trace of a debarred event, of an event whose origin has forever retreated into the void. And this is where the word supercedes itself—and the sentence.

— Finally, the name itself is defined as $μ = \{<μ(β),φ>/β \in α\}$

where $α$: the referential ordinal

$φ$: the minimal condition which always belongs to ♀

the value of $μ$: the set of values of $μ(β)$

(i.e. a canonical name of an element of $\propto$)

Therefore, the value of $μ$ is the set of $β$

Therefore, the value of $μ$ is $α$ itself.

This final series confirms the connectedness and the indexing of a name, $μ$, onto an other name, $α$, whose ♀-referent $μ$ is. And here lies Badiou's insistence on the disobjectifying task of philosophical activity, for a name must here be treated as a full-fledged 'object'.

The underlying assumption to this recognition, however, assumes a split reaction among the characters inhabiting S, namely between the ontologist and the inhabitant of the non-ontological variety. That the indiscernible is supposed to exist will mean two different things according to the group one fits into. For the ontologist, the existence of a generic part of a situation is a certainty (if S is countable, a generic part exists). For the non-ontologist inhabitant of S, the existence of the indiscernible is a matter of theological faith (for '♀' does not belong to S, it is only a part of it). The underlying operation of the canonical names can thus be taken as a recurrence performed directly on membership.

In the demonstration Badiou concludes with two important points. His aim is to materialize with the tools of Set Theory a demonstration which "by the mediation of names appends an indiscernible to a situation where it is indiscernible"—and not transcendent.[15] The fundamental point to retain here is that once a name is appended the generic part *always* belongs to the extension. Otherwise we would have a parallel universe or world, or disjointed planet, but no extension. And this also marks the difference of Badiou's aim in using logic to S. Kripke and H. Putnam's. Badiou seeks not to perfect the nature of reference in this world by way of establishing the logic of a possible or modal world. His act involves spatial connection but temporal deferral. As opposed to Putnam's externalist theory of mind, which he establishes by setting-up a twin planet, Badiou transforms the subject (the reflexive subject of Descartes' theory of mind) by establishing an objectless certainty of the pure multiple indexed to an extension of our fundamental situation. As Badiou states, "The generic extension contains no ordinal which is not already in the fundamental situation. . . . The extension is finally neither more complex nor more natural than the situation. The appending of an indiscernible modifies it only 'a little', precisely because an indiscernible does not add explicit information to the situation in which it is indiscernible."[16]

This notion of truth production as an indiscernible object in S does not suggest approximating or representing what may or may not have occurred at an original site. Approximation and representation

always belong, structurally, to the critical compo-
nents underlying the connection of a truth to an
event, i.e., a pure multiple. Badiou points out that "a
truth contains the following paradox: it is at once
something new, hence something rare and exceptional. Yet, touching the very being of that of which it
is a truth, it is also the most stable, the closest, ontologically speaking, to the initial state of things. This
paradox must be developed at length, but what is
clear is that the *origin* of a truth is of the order of the
event."[17] This conception of philosophy as intervention
involves the discrimination of a given "situation" as a
universe of untotalizable multiplicities, specialist car-
riers of the infinite. Just as there can be no class of
all classes in Set Theory, so also must intervention
accept knowledge of a headless situation. In other
words, neither a member nor a part of the situation
can know it from a transcendent point of view without
feeding the tangled foliage of paradoxes. A truth is
thus, always, the truth of a situation. As such it is
held unbounded by the errant uncountable proliferation of multiplicities.

Situating Truth as operation and separating it
from the production of truths, the stalwart function of
the conditions, are at the heart of what readers will
not mistake as being a system. Badiou updates the
argument that ". . . the systematic vocation is
inevitable and is part of the very essence of philosophy. Obviously if by system we understand theological
systems, architectonics with a keystone, etc., this figure can be said to be inadequate."[18] What makes it
inevitable is that philosophical thinking operates by
sequential argumentative linking matched with random connections which gather together the entire conceptual disposition in thought. To this end, and with a
view to fully describing the relation of philosophy to its

conditions, "it is the same thing to say that philosophy is not systematic and that it *is* not."[19]

As mentioned earlier, Plato lines up the conditions Badiou holds as the basis for philosophy. The condition to which philosophy did not suture itself is love. The lovers of wisdom posit love without a phenomenological object. By the same token, love offers to philosophy the safeguard of immanent disjunction so vital to ground the concept of difference without an object, pure indiscernible difference. Much of French thought over the last three decades has echoed to the sound of this concept. The systematic vocation has not been shared among most of them. Despite its Heideggerian origins in ontico-ontological difference, difference has found widespread applications. Love, though, may just prove to be a stronger warrantor of difference.

Love, explains Badiou, "is the place in which the difference of the sexes, or sexuation, not only is experienced, suffered or spoken, but also given to thought. Sexuation is not simply an empirical phenomenon, but more radically the initial and fundamental scene of difference alone. It is in love that thought is freed from the powers of the One, and operates according to the law of the 'Two', to what breaks into the One."[20] Distinguishing love from sexual longing and giving the former the weight of pure separation suggests that it is not orgasm which pushes sex toward fusion, nor ecstasy, but the panic energy raising the ante of the dominance-submission split.[21] Separation actually emerges as a retroactive move in sex, the splitting of bodies but particularly the splitting from narcissistic fusion, a potentially obsessive act when devoid of the founding properties of the Two which love guarantees in the act. The argument being defended here is meant to offer the tools needed to avoid slipping into the obsessive and dogmatic manic-depressiveness which identification with the One provokes particularly in the sexual couple.[22]

In contrast to this, what mathematics loses in counting power in this system because of the ousting of the One's domination through love's power of the Two, it gains in the clarity of the number as letter of multiplicities. Why renew links with mathematics which since Hegel has been but a distant memory for much of continental philosophy? It is Badiou's conviction that it is within this intimate collaboration that "the pursuit and accomplishment of the process of philosophy's secularization" are at stake.[23] In the nineteenth century, an early effort at re-evoking this link from the point of view of mathematics could be found in Gottlob Frege's thinking on logic. But whereas Frege juxtaposed the function, from math, with the philosophical concept, "a function whose value is always a truth-value", Badiou spots the turnstile elsewhere.[24] There is an intricate relation in his system between Truth and the void by way of being. An idea worthy of foundation is that void is not identical to nothingness. There has been a long perpetuated confusion in philosophy in taking one for the other. The "Axiom of the empty set" from set theory is incorporated as an axiom of this system, demonstrating that the empty set nonetheless does indeed have properties.[25] It is a set to which no member belongs. It can be identified. It can be located. Most of all, and quite unlike nothingness, it can be thought, i.e., it can be separated from Being, if only by name.

Two simultaneous voids operate here. By the very fact of there being more than one of them, void is in no way isomorphic with nothingness. There is the void of the category of Truth. In its emptiness, this void demonstrates not only that philosophy does not have a strict object of study, but also that it does not even produce any truths. This logical dimension gathers together the heterogeneous truths produced by the conditions, assembling them according to a relation of 'compossibility'. Leibniz first spoke of this situation as specific to God's Understanding. Therein, mutually excluded and contradictory properties would not for that matter eliminate the possibilities of juxtaposed and collateral worlds. As this void exists in measured time, the upshot is that only such a model-type manages to gather together apparently disparate truths. On the other hand, on the ontological level, on the level of philosophy's trajectory in any and all historic time-frames whatsoever, thus in an anhistoric time, the void or the empty set is Being itself. As the event arises from chance experience, and disappears just as quickly, it remains only as a trace. Intervening upon this trace comprises the notion of naming, which solidifies the Being of the event by marking it as the undecidable void whose background it is.

Hence, Truth is incapable of being expressed in the sentence, but a truth is, ever since its initial appearance, along with the entire eventful status bestowed unto it by its entering into effectiveness. The event may use the sentence to express its relation of undecidability with respect to measured time. As a process determined by one of the conditions, the event reaches its truth through the determination of a name. This act of intervention is guided by the thoroughly empty category of eternal Truth. Empty because it is an operation and not a substance. On the other side of Hegel, Badiou comes up with Plato today, though both the Greek and German philosophers share the temporal arch endowing the lovers of wisdom with an uncanny contemporaneity throughout the ages.

It is admittedly surprising to find the word 'Manifesto' in the title of a work of philosophy. But a manifesto is nothing without the preposition of its attribute. Political parties and artistic movements alike generate their own manifestos in order to declare their self-existence. It is the pure *of*. Here, the manifesto is aimed at philosophy, it is *for* it, to remind all those sharing in its systems, deconstructions and fictions that the conditions are still conjoined to allow its existence. And that, while philosophy is without its own object of inquiry and transformation, most of its interventions transform the field or object being meditated. Naming is thus the trace of philosophy's intervention upon truths.

The deciding test comes along with confronting that variation of an event which greets no name. The 'unnamable' is both the limit and background of intervention, making the truth procedures possible while establishing its vanishing point. It is the tension in language of philosophy's temptation to transform its empty category of Truth, a pure operation, into substance, worldly or ethereal. What François Wahl calls this system's "ethics of reserve"[26] is the guarantee of the continual permeation of what falls within the situation from without. Naming it can only be committed as a forced act, depleting an outer point of its properties through an overlay of language. Such forcing is tantamount to incarnating the disastrous logic of a will to power into the system itself.

If the philosopher's task is always the breaking of language, which is the mirror in which externally she and the sophist are indiscernible, in Badiou's system it is never to approach or succumb to the unthinkable. Philosophy is thus as such caught in the tension of maintaining the void distinct and separate from substance and "in a constant *reserve* regarding its sophistic double, a reserve thanks to which philosophy is subtracted from the temptation of splitting itself (according to the void-substance couple) in order to deal with the first duplicity founding it (sophist-philosopher)."[27] The elegance of Badiou's rigorous rationalism merely conveys to what extent philosophy's ethics is toward reserve and responsibility.

Be it in the philosophy of mind or questions of the political, philosophy can no longer afford to appeal to the unthinkable as enigma. First, because in suturing itself to any one of its conditions, it hands over to another field the effort of dealing with its own unknowns, a risky option for a field whose original call was to 'know thyself'. Second, quite simply because philosophy has the resources to think its frontiers. It has the tools and concepts—whether other fields have shown that it has or not—to deal with the fissures in language which escape sense. These fissures are the area specific to philosophy where throughout the ages it has contributed most to the evolution of humanity. In embracing the non-human, the anti-human, a strand of French philosophy informs the human, giving it confidence and strength, not to accept depression and nothingness, but to realize that nothingness and void are intrinsically different, and that our enjoyment can only begin upon embracing the void. The void: the dis-appearance of events and sounding for the intervention of naming.

There are a few general remarks to be said about my translation choices. Specific points are tackled in the translation notes, indicated by Roman numerals. Reference footnotes, while few and far between in the original, are indicated by Arabian numerals. Any explicatory notes included among the references to *Manifesto* are my own. (Badiou's begin only with the essays from *Conditions*.)

I have mostly respected Professor Badiou's decision when to highlight concepts by the use of capitals. Though this might not correspond with other English translations of German and French thought, the care with which Badiou tends to define his concepts should erase any ambiguities. Having said this, there is in Badiou's discourse a certain confluence of German Idealist and phenomenological terminology as well as a general debate occurring with the late French psychoanalytic thinker Jacques Lacan. This imposed the need to remain close to current English translations of these traditions, particularly to those of Lacan's proto-linguistics.

For this translation, I am grateful to Professor Badiou for his clarifications and support during the task of casting, as it were, his thought into the English language. I would especially like to thank Professor Thelma Sowley of the Department of Linguistics at University of Paris 8 for the many, many Saturday afternoons she devoted to re-reading and commenting on my manuscript—with only the greatest of rigor. I would also like to express my thanks to Nick Tait, for his secular and professional advice concerning the initial stages of the translation. Ata Hoodashtian first proposed the idea of translating this text and managed to get the proper contacts for publishing it. Professor Jeff Mitscherling from University of Guelph (Canada) and Jed English cleared the final manuscript of my introduction of nasty bugs and gave the go-ahead.

Paris, February 1996

MANIFESTO FOR PHILOSOPHY

1

✳ ✳

POSSIBILITY

The dominant philosophical traditions of the century agree that philosophy, as a discipline, is no longer really what it used to be. It must be said that Carnap's critique of metaphysics as nonsense is very different from Heidegger's announcement of the supersession of metaphysics. It is also very different from the Marxist dream of a concrete realization of philosophy. Very different as well from what Freud ferrets out as illusion, indeed paranoia, from speculative systematicity. But the fact remains that German hermeneutics like Anglo-Saxon analytical philosophy, revolutionary Marxism and psychoanalytical interpretation concur to declare the 'end' of a millennial régime of thought.[i] No further question of imagining a *philosophia perrenis* perpetuating itself.

In this sense, the philosophers of today should rather call themselves 'philosophers'. Most of them say in fact that philosophy is impossible, completed, assigned to something other than itself.

In this respect let us cite the most well-known French philosophers. Philippe Lacoue-Labarthe, for

example: "One must no longer be in desire of philosophy."[1] And almost at the same time, Jean-François
Lyotard: "Philosophy as architecture is ruined."[2] Is it
however possible to imagine a philosophy that is not
in the least architectonic? Is a "writing of ruins", a
"micrologia", a diligence for "graffiti" (which Lyotard
considers as metaphors for the style of contemporary
thought) still connected to 'philosophy', however we
understand it, in any relation other than a simple
homonymic one? What is more: was not the greatest
of our dead, Jacques Lacan, an 'anti-philosopher'?
And how should we interpret the fact that Lyotard
can only evoke the destiny of Presence in commen-
taries on painters, that Gilles Deleuze's last great
book had cinema as its topic, that Lacoue-Labarthe
(like Gadamer in Germany) devotes his energies to
Celan's poetic anticipation, or that Jacques Derrida
calls upon Genet? Almost all our 'philosophers' are in
search of a diverted writing, indirect supports, oblique
referents, so that the evasive transition of a site's
occupation may befall to philosophy's presumably
uninhabitable place. And at the heart of this diversion—the anxious dream of someone who is neither
poet, nor believer nor "Jew"—we find the following,
whetted by the brutal summons of Heidegger's
National-Socialist involvement: in face of the proceed-
ings instituted by our epoch against us and upon
reading the records of this trial, the major evidence of
which is Kolyma and Auschwitz, our philosophers,
taking on the burden of the century and, when it
comes down to it, all of the centuries since Plato, have
decided to *plead guilty*. Neither scientists, a good
many times in the dock, nor the military, nor even
politicians have considered that the massacres of the
century affected them as a body. Sociologists, historians, psychologists, all prosper in innocence. Only phi-

losophers have interiorized the notion that thought,
their thought, encountered the historic[ii] and political
crimes of this century and of all those leading up to it,
both as the obstacle to all continuation and as the tribunal of a collective and historic intellectual forfeiture.

It could of course be thought that there is in this
philosophical singularization of the intellectuality of the
crime, a great deal of conceit. When Lyotard credits
Lacoue-Labarthe with the "first philosophical determination of Nazism", he takes it for granted that such a
determination can be the concern of philosophy. Now,
this is by no means obvious. We know for example
that on no account does the "determination" of the
laws of movement fall within the category of philosophy. I personally maintain that even the ancient
question of being *qua* being does not exclusively fall
within it: it concerns the field of mathematics. It is
thus entirely conceivable that the determination of
Nazism—for example, of Nazism as political—be
removed *de jure* from the specific form of thinking
which, since Plato, has deserved the name of philosophy. Our modest partisans of the impasse of philosophy could well maintain—or detain—persistence
in the idea that 'everything' is the concern of philosophy. From this speculative totalitarianism, it must
indeed be recognized that Heidegger's National-
Socialist involvement was one of its outcomes. What
in fact did Heidegger do other than presume that the
"firm resolve" of the German people as embodied by
the Nazis was transitive to his thinking as a professor and hermeneutician? To posit that philosophy—
and philosophy alone—is accountable for the
sublime or repugnant avatars of the political[iii] in the
century is somewhat similar to the Hegelian ruse of
Reason lurking in the most intimate corners of our
anti-dialecticians' apparatuses. It is to postulate an

essential determination, namely that a Zeitgeist exists, of which philosophy is the principle of capture and concentration. Instead, let us begin by imagining that, for example, Nazism is not as such a possible object for philosophy, that it is not part of the conditions which philosophical thought is authentically able to configurate within its own order. That it is not an event addressed by this thinking. Which does not in any way suggest it is unthinkable.

For conceit turns into a dangerous deficiency when our philosophers, from the axiom putting the accusation of the crimes of the century at philosophy's door, draw the joint conclusions of philosophy's impasse and the unthinkable nature of the crime. For whoever supposes that the extermination of European Jews must be philosophically evaluated from the standpoint of Heidegger's thinking, the impasse is in fact blatant. One can get out of this impasse by exposing that, here, there is some unthinkable, some inexplicable, some rubble for any concept. One will be ready to sacrifice philosophy itself to preserve this conceit: since philosophy must think Nazism and that it has not the means to do so. What it must think is unthinkable, namely that philosophy is in the pass of an impasse.

I suggest we sacrifice the imperative and declare that: if philosophy is incapable of conceptualizing the extermination of European Jews, it is the fact that it is neither its duty nor within its power to conceptualize it. It is up to an *other order of thought* to render *this* thinking actual. For example, the thinking of historicity, that is, of History examined from the standpoint of the political.

It is never really modest to declare an 'end', a completion, a radical impasse. The announcement of the 'End of the Grand Narratives' is as immodest as the

Grand Narrative itself, the certainty of the 'end of meta-physics' proceeds within the metaphysical element of certainty, the deconstruction of the concept of subject requires a central category—being, for example—the historical prescription of which is even more decisive, etc. Overcome by the tragic nature of its supposed object—the extermination, the camps—philosophy transfigures its own impossibility into a prophetic posture. It adopts the somber colors of the time, heedless that this aesthetization is *also* an offense against the victims. The contrite prosopopoeia of abjection is as much a posture, an imposture, as the bugle blaring cavalry of the Spirit's second coming. The end of the End of History is cut from the same cloth as this End.

Once philosophy's stakes have been delimited, the pathos of its 'end' gives way to quite another question, which is the one of its conditions. I do not claim that philosophy is possible at every moment. I propose a general examination of the conditions under which it is possible, in accordance with its destination. That history's violence can interrupt it is an idea which cannot be given credence without closer examination. It would be to concede a strange victory to Hitler and his henchmen to declare outright that they had managed to introduce the unthinkable into thought and so terminated its 'architectured' exercise. Must we grant the fanatical anti-intellectualism of the Nazis this vengeance following its crushing military defeat, namely that thought itself, be it philosophical or political, is in effect incapable of taking stock of the force which intended to annihilate it? Let me make myself clear: it would be tantamount to making the Jews die a second time if their death brought about the end of the fields to which they decisively con-tributed, revolutionary politics on the one hand, ratio-nalist philosophy on the other. The most essential reverence toward the victims cannot reside in the mind's stupor, in its self-accusatory vacillation in face of the crime. It always resides in the *continuation* of what designated them as representatives of Humanity in the eyes of their murderers.

I postulate not only that philosophy is possible today, but that this possibility does not take the form of a final stage. On the contrary, the crux of the matter is to know what the following means: taking *one more step*. A single step. A step within the modern configuration, the one that since Descartes has bound the three nodal concepts of being, truth and the subject to the conditions of philosophy.

2

＊＊

CONDITIONS

Philosophy has begun; it does not exist within all historic configurations; its way of being is discontinuity in time as in space. It must thus be presupposed that it requires particular conditions. If one measures the distance between Greek city-states, classical Western absolute monarchies and bourgeois parliamentary societies, it appears at once that all hope of determining the conditions of philosophy from the mere objective plinth of 'social formations' or even from the great ideological, religious or mythical discourses is doomed to fail. The conditions of philosophy are transversal. They are uniform procedures recognizable from afar, whose relation to thought is relatively invariant. The *name* of this invariance is clear: it is the name 'truth'. The procedures that condition philosophy are truth procedures, identifiable as such in their recurrence. We can no longer believe the narratives by which a human group invokes its origin or destiny. We know that Olympia is only a hill and the Sky is filled only with hydrogen or helium. But that the series of prime numbers is unlimited may be demonstrated today exactly as in Euclid's *Elements*,

33

that Phidias[i] was a great sculptor is not in doubt, that Athenian democracy was a political invention whose theme still occupies us and that love designates the occurrence of a Two in which the subject is trans-fixed—this we understand when reading Sappho or Plato just as when reading Corneille or Beckett.

However, all of this did not always exist. There are societies without mathematics, others in which 'art', in coalescence with obsolete sacred functions, is opaque for us, others in which love is absent, or unutterable, others finally in which despotism has never yielded to political invention nor even tolerated that it be thinkable. Still less have these procedures existed *together* from time immemorial. If Greece saw the birth of philosophy, it is certainly not because it held the Sacred within the mythical resource of the poem, nor because the veiling of Presence was famil-iar to it in the guise of an esoteric statement about being. Many other ancient civilizations proceeded to the sacral depositing of being within poetic utterance. The singularity of Greece is much rather to have *inter-rupted* the narrative about origins through secular-ized and abstract statements, to have impaired the prestige of the poem in favor of that of the matheme[ii], to have conceived the Polis as an open, disputed, vacant power and to have brought the storms of pas-sion to the stage.

The first philosophical configuration that pro-poses to dispose these procedures—the set of these procedures—, in a unique conceptual space, thus showing that *in thought* they are compossible, is the one that bears the name Plato.[iii] "Let no one enter here who is not a geometer", prescribes the matheme as a condition of philosophy.[iv] The distressing dis-missal of the poets, banished from the Polis on grounds of imitation—let us understand: of an overly sensible capture of the Idea—indicates both that the poem is at fault and that it must be measured against the inescapable interruption of the narrative. Concerning love, the *Symposium* and the *Pheado* give its articulation to truth in unsurpassable texts. Political invention is finally set forth as the very texture of thought: at the end of Book IX of the *Republic*, Plato explicitly indicates that his ideal Polis is neither a program nor a reality, that the question of knowing whether it exists or can exist is irrelevant, and hence it is not a matter of politics, but of the political as a condition of thought, of the intra-philosophical formulation of the reasons for which there is no philosophy without the political possessing the real status of a possible invention.

We shall thus posit that there are four conditions of philosophy, and that the lack of a single one gives rise to its dissipation, just as the emergence of all four conditioned its apparition. These conditions are: the matheme, the poem, political invention and love. We shall call the set of these conditions *generic procedures*, for reasons to which I shall later return and that are at the heart of *L'Etre et l'événement*.[1] According to these same reasons, the four types of generic procedures specify and class all the procedures determined thus far which may produce truths (there are but scientific, artistic, political and amorous truths). We can therefore say that philosophy requires there to be truths within each of the orders in which they may be invoked.

Two problems then arise. First, if philosophy has truth procedures as conditions, this signifies that it does not itself produce truths. In fact, this situation is quite well-known; who can cite a single philosophical statement which one can meaningfully say is 'true'?

But then, what exactly is at stake in philosophy? Secondly, we assume that philosophy is 'one' in that it is valid to speak of 'Philosophy' in general, to recognize a text as philosophical. What relation does this presumed unity maintain with the plurality of conditions? What is the nexus of the four (the generic procedures: matheme, poem, political invention and love) and the one (philosophy)? I shall show that these two problems have a sole answer contained within the definition of philosophy, such that it is here represented as an unactual veracity under the condition of the actuality of the true.

The truth or generic procedures stand out from the cumulation of fields of knowledge by their *eventful origin.*[v] As long as nothing happens, aside from that which conforms to the rules of a state of things, there can admittedly be cognition, correct statements, accumulated knowledge; there cannot be truth. A truth contains the following paradox: it is at once something new, hence something rare and exceptional, yet, touching the very being of that of which it is a truth, it is also the most stable, the closest, ontologically speaking, to the initial state of things. This paradox must be developed at length, but what is clear is that the *origin* of a truth is of the order of the event.

In the interests of brevity, let us call 'situation', a state of things, any presented multiple whatsoever. In order that a truth procedure relative to a situation deploy itself, a pure event must supplement this situation. This supplement can neither be named nor represented by referring to the resources of the situation (its structure, the established language naming its terms, etc.). It is inscribed by a singular naming, the bringing into play of an *additional signifier*. And it is the effects *on the situation* of this bringing into play of an 'additional-name' which will weave a generic procedure and set the suspension of a truth *of* the situation. For, in the beginning, in the situation, if no event supplements it there is no truth. There is merely what I call veridicality. Diagonally, through gaps, out of all the veridical statements, there is a chance that a truth befall from the moment that an event has encountered its supernumerary name.

The specific role of philosophy is to propose a unified conceptual space in which naming *takes place* of events that serve as the point of departure for truth procedures. Philosophy seeks to *gather together all the additional-names*. It deals within thought with the compossible nature of the procedures that condition it. It does not establish any truth but it sets a locus of truths. It configurates the generic procedures, through a welcoming, a sheltering, built up with reference to their disparate simultaneity. Philosophy sets out to think its time by putting the state of procedures conditioning it into a common place. Its operations, whatever they may be, always aim to think 'together', to configurate within an unique exercise of thought the epochal disposition of the matheme, poem, political invention and love (or the event status of the Two). In this sense, philosophy's sole question is indeed that of the truth. Not that it produces any, but because it offers a mode of access to the unity of a moment of truths, a conceptual site in which the generic procedures are thought of as compossible.

Of course, the philosophical operators must not be understood as summations, totalizations. The eventful and heterogeneous nature of the four types of truth procedures entirely excludes their encyclopedic alignment. The encyclopedia is a dimension of knowledge, not of truth, the latter creating a hole in knowledge. It is not even always necessary that philosophy *bring up* the statements or local states of generic procedures. Philosophical concepts weave a general space in which thought accedes to time, to *its* time, so long as the truth procedures of this time find shelter for their compossibility within it. The appropriate metaphor is thus not of the register of addition, not even of systematic reflection. It is rather of the liberty of movement, of a moving-itself of thought within the articulated element of a state of its conditions. Within philosophy's conceptual medium, local figures as intrinsically heterogeneous as those of the poem, matheme, political invention and love are related, or may be related to the singularity of time. Philosophy does not pronounce truth but its *conjuncture*, that is, the thinkable conjunction of truths.

Since philosophy is an exercise of thinking about the breach in time, a reflecting torsion about that which conditions it, it most often sustains itself through precarious, nascent conditions. It sets itself up on the outskirts of the intervening naming through which an event sets a generic procedure in motion. The conditioning of a great philosophy, at the furthest reaches of instituted and consolidated knowledge, is carried out by the crises, breakthroughs and paradoxes of mathematics, the quaking of poetic language, the revolutions and provocations of inventive politics, the wavering of the relation between the two sexes. Anticipating to some extent the welcoming and sheltering of these fragile procedures in thought, disposing of trajectories as compossible, of which the mere possibility is still not firmly established, philosophy compounds problems. Heidegger is quite correct to write that "it is certainly philosophy's authentic task to compound, to make the (in this case, historical) Being-there heavier", since "compounding is one of the decisive fundamental conditions for the birth of all that is great."[2] Even if we set ambiguities about "greatness" aside, it may be said that philosophy overloads the 'possible' of truths by its concept of the compossible. Its "compounding" function is to set the generic procedures in the dimension not of their own thinking, but of their joint historicity.

Philosophy configurates the becoming-disparate of the system of its conditions by construction of a space of thoughts of the time. As seen by this system, philosophy serves as a passage between the procedural actuality of truths and the open question of their temporal being.

3

* *

MODERNITY

The conceptual operators by which philosophy configurates its conditions generally place thinking about time under the paradigm of one or several of these conditions. A generic procedure, close to its original eventful site, or confronted by the impasses of its persistence, serves as the main referent for the deployment of the compossibility of the conditions. Thus, within the context of the political crisis of the Greek city-states and of the 'geometrical' re-shaping–after Eudoxus–of the theory of sizes[1], Plato set out to turn mathematics and the political, the theory of proportions and the Polis as an imperative, into the axial referents of a space of thinking whose exercising function was designated by the word 'dialectic'.

How are mathematics and the political ontologically compossible? Such was the Platonic question to which the operator of the Form came to provide the main fulcrum of a resolution. Suddenly, poetry found itself stricken with suspicion–but this suspicion is a receivable form of configuration. And, love, following Plato's own expression, was to bind the 'suddenly' of an encounter with the fact that a truth-here, that of

Beauty-befall as indiscernible, being neither discourse (*logos*) nor knowledge (*epistémè*).

We shall agree to call a 'period' of philosophy a sequence of its existence for which a certain configuration, specified by a dominant condition, persists. Throughout such a period, the operators of compossibility depend on this specification. A period creates a nexus out of the four generic procedures, in the singular, post-eventful state in which they are found. This post-eventful state is under the jurisdiction of concepts through which a generic procedure is inscribed into the space of thinking and circulation that philosophically serves as the determination of the time. In the Platonic example, the Form is manifestly an operator whose 'true' underlying principal is the matheme. The political is invented as a condition of thought under the jurisdiction of the Form (whence the philosopher-king, and the remarkable role played by arithmetic and geometry in this king or guardian's education). Imitative poetry is held at bay, the more so, as shown by Plato in the *Gorgias* as much as in the *Protagoras*, inasmuch as there is a paradoxical complicity between poetry and sophistry: poetry is the secret, esoteric dimension of sophistry since it carries to the highest point language's flexibility and variance.

Thus the question for us is as follows: Is there a *modern* period of philosophy? Today, the acuity of this question is attributed to the fact that the majority of philosophers declare, on the one hand, that there is indeed such a period, and on the other, that we are contemporaries of its completion. This is the meaning of the expression 'postmodern'. But even for those who use this expression sparingly, the theme of an 'end' of philosophical modernity, of a depletion of operators that are its very own-especially the category of Subject-is always present, albeit under the schemata of the end of metaphysics. Most of the time moreover this end is ascribed to the Nietzschean utterance.

If one empirically designates 'Modern Times' by the period that stretches from the Renaissance till today, it is certainly difficult to speak of a period, in the sense of a hierarchical invariance in the philosophical configuration of the conditions. It is in fact clear:

— that in Europe's Classical age, the era of Descartes and Leibniz, the mathematical condition was dominant, under the effect of the Galilean event, whose essence was the introduction of the infinite into the matheme;

— that starting from Rousseau and Hegel, underscored by the French Revolution, the compossibility of the generic procedures is under the jurisdiction of the historico-political condition;

— that between Nietzsche and Heidegger, art, whose heart is the poem, made a return, through an anti-Platonic retroaction, in the operators by which philosophy designated our time as that of a forgetful nihilism.

Thus, throughout this temporal sequence, there is a displacement of the order, of the principal referent from which the compossibility of the generic procedures is drawn. The *coloration* of these concepts bears good witness to this displacement, between the order of Cartesian concepts, the temporal pathos of the concept with Hegel and Heidegger's meta-poetic metaphorizing.

Yet, this displacement must not conceal the invariance, at least till Nietzsche but pursued and extended by Freud and Lacan as well as Husserl, of the theme of the Subject. This theme only endures a radical deconstruction in Heidegger's work and that of his successors. The recasting to which it is subjected by Marxist politics and by psychoanalysis (which is the modern treatment of the condition of love) is related to the historicity of the conditions, and not to the termination of the philosophic operator dealing with this historicity.

It is thus convenient to define philosophy's modern period by the central organizational use to which the category of Subject is put. Although this category does not prescribe a kind of configuration, a stable régime of compossibility, it is sufficient as far as formulating the following question is concerned: Is the modern period of philosophy over? Which is akin to saying: Does the act of proposing, for our time, a space of compossibility within thought of the truths which proliferate there, demand the maintenance and usage of the category of Subject, even profoundly altered or subverted? Or, on the contrary, is our time one in which thought demands the deconstruction of this category? To this question, Lacan replied with a radical reorganization of a maintained category (which means that for him the modern period of philosophy continues, which is also Christian Jambet's perspective, Guy Lardreau's and my own). Heidegger (but also Deleuze with some nuances, Lyotard, Derrida, Lacoue-Labarthe and Jean-Luc Nancy vigorously) replies that our epoch is the one in which "subjectivity is driven toward its completion."[1] To this, he adds that, consequently, thought can complete itself only over and above this "completion", which is none other than the destructive objectivation of the Earth; that the category of Subject must be deconstructed and held as the ultimate (modern, precisely) avatar of metaphysics; and that the philosophical apparatus of rational thought, whose central operator is this category, is now held to such a degree in the unfathomable oblivion of that which founds it that "thinking shall only begin once we have learned that this thing, Reason, which has been so magnified for centuries, is the most relentless enemy of thought."[2]

Are we still, and if so on what grounds, Galilean and Cartesian? Are Reason and the Subject still apt to serve as vectors of the configurations of philosophy, even if the Subject is 'eccentric' or void, and Reason subjected to the supernumerary chance of the event? Is truth the veiled non-veiledness whose risk only the poem receives in words? Or is it that by which philosophy designates, within its own space, the disjointed generic procedures that plait together the obscure continuation of Modern Times? Must we continue, or must we be in possession of the meditation of an awaiting? Such is the only significant polemical question today: to decide if the form of thinking about Time, philosophically reared by the events of love, the poem, the matheme and inventive politics, remains bound to the disposition which Husserl still named the "Cartesian meditation".

4

**

HEIDEGGER VIEWED
AS COMMONPLACE

What does the 'current' Heidegger say, the one who organizes opinion? He says the following:

1) The modern figure of metaphysics, such that it has been articulated around the category of Subject, is in the epoch of its completion. The veritable sense of the category of Subject is rendered in the universal process of objectivation, a process whose appropriated name is: the reign of technology. The becoming-subject of Man is merely the ultimate metaphysical transcription of the establishment of this reign: "The very fact that man becomes subject and the world object is but the consequence of the essence of technology which is in the process of being installed."[1] Indeed, inasmuch as it is an effect of the planetary deployment of technology, the category of Subject is incapable of turning thought back toward the essence of this deployment. Thinking technology as the ultimate historical metamorphosis, and closure, of the epoch of the metaphysics of Being is the only possible program today for thought in and of itself. Thought

cannot thus establish its site from that which the category of Subject enjoins us to hold: this injunction is indistinguishable from technology's.

2) The planetary reign of technology brings about the end of philosophy; within it the possibilities of philosophy, i.e., of metaphysics, are irreversibly depleted. Our time is no longer exactly "modern", if by "modern" we understand the post-Cartesian configuration of metaphysics, which has organized the predominance of the Subject or of Consciousness over the disposition of the philosophic text up to Nietzsche. For our time is that of the *execution* of the ultimate figure of metaphysics, that of the depletion of what is possible for metaphysics to do. And consequently, that of the 'in-different' expansion of technology, whose representation is no longer bound to philosophy, for within technology, philosophy, or more precisely what philosophy possessed and signified regarding the potency of Being, attained completion as the Earth's devastating will.

3) The technological completion of metaphysics, whose two main "necessary consequences" are modern science and the totalitarian State, can and must be ascertained by thought as nihilism, i.e., as the very execution of non-thought. Technology carries non-thought to its peak for, as regards thinking, there is but thinking of Being, and technology is the ultimate destiny of the hiddenness[i] of Being within the strict consideration of the existent.[ii] Technology is in fact a willing, a relation to Being whose forgetful forcing is essential since it realizes the will to subjugate existents *in their totality*. Technology is the will to enframe[iii] and to hold onto the existent such that it is 'there', as a limitless depth available to enslaving

manipulation. The only "concept" of being known to technology is *raw material*, which is proposed without reservations to the forcing of an unleashed willing-to-produce and willing-to-destroy. The will as viewed by the existent, which constitutes the essence of technology, is nihilistic in that it *processes* the existent without the least regard for the thinking of its being and in such obliviousness of Being it is rendered forgetful to that very obliviousness. The upshot of this is that the willing that is immanent to technology summons the being of the existent to nothingness, which it processes entirely. The will to enframe and to hold is exactly the same thing as the will to annihilate. The total destruction of the Earth is the *necessary* horizon of technology not for the particular reason that any given practice exists that institutes this risk, military or nuclear practice, for example, but because the essence of technology is to mobilize Being, brutally treated as a simple reserve of availability for willing in the latent and essential form of nothingness.

Our time is thus nihilistic if we question it as to thought as well as to the destiny of Being it deploys. As regards thought, our time is steered away from it by the radical overshadowing of unconcealedness[iv], the letting-be conditioning its exercise and the undivided reign of willing. As regards Being, our time vows it to annihilation. Or rather: Being itself passes on from its 'pro-position' as nothingness once it proliferates, withdrawn and subtracted, solely in the closing of raw material and in the technological availability of an unfathomable depth.

4) In the modern age (in which man becomes Subject and the world Object due to the establishing of the reign of technology) and after in our time of unleashed objectifying technology, a few poets alone

have pronounced being. Or a few have at least pronounced the conditions of a turnabout of thought, out of the subjective prescription of technological willing toward unconcealedness and the Disclosed. The poetic voice—and it alone—ᵛ has rung out as a possible *foundation* for a gathering-together of the Disclosed against the infinite and closed availability of the existent with which technology deals. These poets are Hölderlin, the unsurpassable, then Rilke and Trakl. The poetic word of these poets has made holes in the fabric of oblivion. It has detained—preserved—, not Being itself, whose historical destiny reaches completion in the distress of our time, but the *question* of Being. Poets have been the shepherds, the vigils of this question which the reign of technology renders universally unpronounceable.

5) Philosophy has attained completion. All that is left to us is to pronounce the question again over which the poets stand guard, and to grasp how this question has rung out throughout the entire course of the history of philosophy since its Greek origins. Thought is today *under the poets' condition*. Under this condition it turns back toward interpretation of the origins of philosophy, toward the first gestures of metaphysics. It seeks out the keys to its own destiny, to its own actual completion, in the *first step of oblivion*. That first step of oblivion is Plato. Analysis of the Platonic "turning" as regards the bond between Being and Truth dictates the seizing of the historical destiny of Being, which reaches completion before our eyes in the provocation to annihilate. The heart of this "turning" is the interpretation of Truth and Being as Form, that is, the termination of the poem, to the benefit of— putting it into my own language here—the matheme. The Platonic interruption of the poetic and metaphoric

narrative by the paradigmatic ideal of the matheme-
Heidegger interprets this as the inaugural orientation
of the destiny of Being toward the forgetting of its
unconcealedness, the relinquishing of its initial appro-
priateness to the Greeks' poetic language. Therefore
we may just as well say that the retracing toward the
origin, such that it today obtains its condition from
the word of the poets, reverts to the word of the Greek
poets, pre-Platonic thinker-poets who still maintained
the tension between disclosedness and the veiled
unconcealedness of Being.

6) The threefold movement of thought is thus the
following: taking up a condition in the word of the
poets; interpretive retracing toward the Platonic turning that dictated the metaphysical epoch of Being;
exegesis of the Presocratic origin of thought. By
means of this threefold movement one may put forth
the hypothesis of a return of the Gods, of an *event*
wherein the mortal danger to which the annihilating
will exposes Man—technology's civil servant—would
be surpassed or conjured away by a *sheltering* of
Being, a re-exposure to the thinking of its destiny as
disclosedness and unconcealedness, and not as the
unfathomable depths of the availability of existents.
This presupposition of a return of the Gods can be
stated by the thinking that poets teach, it obviously
cannot be *announced.* To say "only a God can save
us" means: the thinking that poets teach—educated
by cognition of the Platonic turning, renewed by interpretation of the Presocratic Greeks—may uphold at
the heart of nihilism the possibility, devoid of any way
or means open to utterance, of a resacralization of the
Earth.[2] Here, "to save" is not to be taken in the soft
sense of a soul supplement. "To save" means: to steer
Man and the Earth away from annihilation, an anni-

hilation that Being, in the terminal technical figure of its destiny, has as its being to *will*. The God in question is the god of the diversion of a destiny. It is not a question of saving the soul, but of saving Being, of saving it from that which alone can put it into peril, and which is itself in the implacable terminal prescription of its historicity. This self-salvation within Being imposes on one to venture to the ends of distress, hence to the ends of technology, to risk the diversion. For only in the most extreme of perils does what saves also grow.

5

* *

NIHILISM?

We shall not accept that the word 'technology'—
even were we to resonate the Greek *tekhnè* within it—
is apt to designate the essence of our time, nor that
there be any relation useful to thought between 'technology's planetary reign' and 'nihilism'. The meditations, calculations and diatribes about technology,
widespread though they are, are nonetheless uni-
formly ridiculous. And we must loudly proclaim what
many refined Heideggerians think in private:
Heidegger's texts on this point do not in any way
avoid this pomposity. The "timber trail", the clear-
eyed peasant, the Earth's devastation, the rooting in a
natural site, the blossoming of the rose, all this
pathos, from Alfred de Vigny ("on this steel bull that
smokes and bellows, man has mounted too soon"[1]) to
our 'publicists', by way of Georges Duhamel and
Giono, are spun only from reactionary nostalgia. The
stereotyped nature of these ruminations, a matter of
what Marx called "feudal socialism", is moreover the
best proof of their meager conceivable sense.

If I had to give my opinion on technology, whose
relation to the contemporary demands of philosophy

is fairly scant, it would much rather be to regret that it is still so mediocre, so timid. So many useful instruments do not exist or only exist in heavy and inconvenient forms! So many major adventures get nowhere or are of the 'life-is-too-slow' type. Just look at planetary exploration, energy through thermo-nuclear fusion, flying machines for everyone, three-dimensional images... We must indeed say: 'Gentlemen Technicians, one more effort if you are truly working towards the planetary reign of technology!' Not enough technology, technology that is still very rudi-mentary—that is the real situation: the reign of Capital bridles and simplifies technology whose 'virtu-alities' are infinite.

Besides, it is completely inappropriate to present science as belonging to the same register in terms of thought as technology. There is certainly a relation of necessity between science and technology but it does not imply any community of interests. The statements displaying 'modern science' as the *effect*, indeed the main effect of technology's reign, are untenable. If, for example, we consider a very great theorem from mod-ern mathematics, the one that demonstrates the inde-pendence of the Continuum Hypothesis (Paul Cohen, 1963), we find within it a concentration of thought, an inventive beauty, a surprise of the concept, a risky rupture, in a nutshell, an intellectual aesthetic that we can, if we so choose, compare to the greatest poems of our century, to the politico-military audacity of a revolutionary stratagem, or to the most intense emotions of an amorous encounter, but certainly not to an electric coffee grinder or a color television, as useful and ingenious as these objects may be. Science, *qua* science, that is, grasped in its truth pro-cedure is, moreover, profoundly *useless*, save that it avers thought as such in an unconditioned way.

There is no turning back on the statement made by the Greeks (the uselessness of science, except as a pure exercise and generic condition of thought), even under the fallacious pretext that Greek society was a slave-society. The dogma of utility always amounts to excusing the fact that one does not really want—what is called willing—*uselessness for all.*

As for 'nihilism', we shall acknowledge that our epoch bears witness to it precisely in the way that by nihilism we understand the *rupture of the traditional figure of the bond,* un-binding as a form of being of all that pretends to be of the bond.[1] Our time indubitably sustains itself with a kind of generalized atomism because no symbolic sanction of the bond is capable of resisting the abstract potency of Capital. That everything that is *bound up* proves that in terms of being it is unbound; that the reign of the multiple is the unfathomable depths of what is presented without exception; that the One is but the result of transitory operations—there lies the inescapable effect of the universal placing of the terms of our situation within the circulating movement of the general monetary equivalent. Just as what presents itself always has a temporal substance, and that time is literally *counted* for us, so nothing exists which is intrinsically bound to something else, since each of the terms of this supposed essential binding are projected indifferently onto the neutral surface of computation. There is absolutely nothing to review of the description given of this state of things one hundred and forty-eight years ago by Marx:

"The bourgeoisie, wherever it has got the upper hand, has put an end to all feudal, patriarchal, idyllic relations. It has pitilessly torn asunder the motley feudal bonds that unite man to his 'natural superiors', and has left remaining no other bonds between man and man than naked self-interest, callous 'cash payment'. It has drowned the most heavenly ecstasies of religious fervor, of chivalrous enthusiasm, of philistine sentimentalism, in the icy water of egotistical calculation."[2]

What Marx brings to the fore is especially the end of the *sacred* figures of the bond, the lapsing of the symbolic guarantee granted to the bond by productive and monetary stagnation. Capital is the general dissolvent of sacralizing representations, which postulate the existence of intrinsic and essential relations (between man and nature, men, groups and the Polis, mortal and eternal life, etc.). It is altogether typical that the denunciation of 'technological nihilism' is always correlated to the nostalgia of such relations. The disappearance of the sacred is a recurrent theme with Heidegger himself, and the prediction of its return is identified with the theme, borrowed from Hölderlin, of the "return of the Gods". If one takes 'nihilism' to mean desacralization, Capital, whose planetary reign is beyond any doubt—'technology' and 'Capital' being only paired off in an historic sequence but not in the concept—is certainly the only nihilistic potency of which men have succeeded in being the inventors as well as the prey.

Yet, for Marx, and for us, desacralization is not in the least nihilistic, insofar as 'nihilism' must signify that which declares that the access to being and truth is impossible. On the contrary, desacralization is a *necessary condition* for the disclosing of such an approach to thought. It is obviously the only thing we can and must welcome within Capital: it exposes the pure multiple as the foundation of presentation; it denounces every effect of One as a simple, precarious configuration; it dismisses the symbolic representations in which the bond found a semblance of being.

That this destitution operates in the most complete barbarity must not conceal its properly *ontological* virtue. To whom must we be grateful to be delivered from the myth of Presence, the guarantee which it grants to the substantiality of the bonds and to the durability of essential relations, if not to the roaming automaticity of Capital? To think over and above Capital and its mediocre prescription (the general computation of time), we must still have as *a departure point* what it has revealed: Being is essentially multiple, sacred Presence is a pure semblance and truth, as with anything if it exists, is not a revelation, much less so the proximity of that which withdraws itself. It is a regulated procedure resulting in a supplementary multiple.

Our epoch is neither technical (for it is so with mediocrity) nor nihilistic (for it is the first one that the destitution of sacred bonds lays open to the genericity of the true). Its own enigma, against the grain of the nostalgic speculations of feudal socialism whose most complete emblem has certainly been Hitler, resides first in the local maintenance of the sacred which has been attempted, but also denied, by the great poets since Hölderlin. And, second, in the anti-technological, archaistic reactions which continue to secure together under our very eyes the debris of religion (from the soul supplement to Islamism), messianic politics (including Marxism), occult sciences (astrology, healing plants, telepathic massages, tickle and touch group therapy) and all types of pseudo-bonds for which the syrupy love exalted in songs—loveless, truthless and encounterless love—constitutes the flaccid universal matrix.

Philosophy is not by any means complete. But the stubbornness of these residues of the One's empire, which constitute anti-'nihilistic' nihilism, since they

place themselves abeam to truth procedures and designate the recurrent *obstacle* opposed to subtractive
ontology—Capital being its historic medium—leads us
to think that philosophy has been in *abeyance* for a
long time.

I shall put forth this paradox: philosophy has not
known until quite recently how to think *in level terms
with Capital*, since it has left the field open, to its
most intimate point, to vain nostalgia for the sacred,
to obsession with Presence, to the obscure dominance
of the poem, to doubt about its own legitimacy. It has
not known how to *make thought out of* the fact that
man has become irreversibly 'master and possessor of
nature' and that it is here neither a matter of loss nor
of oblivion, but of its supreme destination—albeit fea-
tured, still, in the stupid opacity of computed time.
Philosophy has left the 'Cartesian meditation' incom-
plete by going astray in the aestheticization of willing
and the pathos of completion, the destiny of oblivion
and the lost trace. It has not cared to recognize in a
straightforward way the absoluteness of the multiple
and the non-being of the bond. It has clung to language, to literature, to *writing* just as to the last possible representatives of an *a priori* determination of
experience, or to the preserved place of a clearing of
Being. It has declared since Nietzsche that what had
begun with Plato was reaching its twilight, but this
arrogant declaration concealed the powerlessness to
continue this beginning. Philosophy denounces or
showers praise upon 'nihilistic modernity' only to the
extent of the difficulty it has itself in grasping where
current positivities pass in transit, and given its inability to conceive that we have blindly entered into a new
phase of the doctrine of Truth, that of the multiple-
without-One, or of fragmentary, infinite and indiscernible totalities. 'Nihilism' is a least-worst signifier.

The true question remains: What has happened to philosophy for it to refuse with a shudder the liberty and strength a desacralizing epoch offered it?

6

**

SUTURES

If philosophy is, as I defend it to be, the configuration, within thought, of the fact that its four generic conditions (the poem, the matheme, the political and love) are compossible *in the eventful form prescribing the truths of the time*, a suspension of philosophy can result from the restriction or blockage of the free play required in order to define a regime of passage, or of intellectual circulation between the truth procedures conditioning philosophy. The most frequent cause of such blockage is that instead of constructing a space of compossibility through which the thinking of time is practiced, philosophy *delegates* its functions to one or other of its conditions, handing over the whole of thought to *one* generic procedure. Philosophy is then carried out in the element of its own suppression to the great benefit of that procedure.

I shall call this type of situation a *suture*. Philosophy is placed in suspension every time it presents itself as being sutured to one of its conditions. For this reason, philosophy is forbidden to freely construct a *sui generis* space wherein eventful naming, indicating the novelty of the four conditions, come to

be inscribed and aver, in an exercise of thinking distinct from all of the conditions, their simultaneity and
thus a certain configurable state of the truths of the
epoch.

The nineteenth century, from Hegel to Nietzsche,
was largely dominated by sutures, and this is why,
during that period, philosophy seems to have been
subjected to an eclipse. The main suture was the *positivist* or scientistic suture, which expected science to
configurate on its own the completed system of truths
of the time. This suture still dominates academic
Anglo-Saxon philosophy, although its prestige has
worn thin. Its most visible effects are naturally cen-
tered on the status of the other conditions. As regards
the political condition, it finds itself withdrawn from
any eventful status, reduced as it is to the pragmatic
defense of the liberal-parliamentarian regime. The
latent as well as central statement is in fact that the
political *in no way is the concern of thought*. The
poetic condition is debarred, filed under the cultural
supplement or proposed as an object for linguistic
analyses. The amorous condition is ignored: I owe
Jean-Luc Nancy the profound remark that the
essence of the USA is to be a country in which sentimentality and sex coexist at the expense of love. The
suture of philosophy to its scientific condition progressively reduces it to be but mere analytic quibbling, whose language *bears the brunt* in every sense
of the term. Free reign is thus given to a diffuse reli-
giosity, which serves as a cotton dressing for the cuts
and bumps of capitalist brutality.

In its dominant canonical form, Marxism itself has
proposed a suture, the suture of philosophy to its political condition. This is the idea behind the whole equivocation concerning the famous thesis on Feuerbach,
which claims to substitute to the "interpretation" of the

world, its revolutionary transformation. Here, the political is *philosophically* designated as alone apt to practically configurate the general system of sense, and philosophy is doomed to its fructifying suppression. That the political, moreover well identified by Marx with the real movement of History, should be the ultimate form of the totalization of experience, simultaneously dismisses the other conditions and the philosophy that claimed to inscribe on that experience its compossibility with the political. We are familiar with Marx and the Marxists' setbacks as far as artistic activity is concerned, unable as they were to think its singularity or respect its inventive rigor. As for the truth effects of sexual difference[i], they were subjected, all things considered, to the double occultation of 'socialist' Puritanism and the scorn in which psychoanalysis was held (which is, to my mind, the only true modern attempt to make a concept out of love).

For the scientific condition, the matter is more complex. Marx and his successors, in this way products of the dominant positivist suture, always claimed to raise revolutionary politics to the rank of a science. They maintained the equivocation between the "science of History"—historical materialism[ii]—and the mastered movement of History from the angle of the political. Right from the start, they opposed their "scientific" socialism to diverse "utopian" ones. It can thus be argued that Marxism *crossed* two sutures, to the political and to science. It is, moreover, the complex network of this double suturation that Stalin in particular calls "philosophy"—or dialectical materialism. The upshot of this is that the said "philosophy" is presented in the strange form of "laws", the "laws of dialectics", equivocally applicable to Nature and to History.

But in the final analysis, as in the "materialist" vision, science is sent back to its technico-historic conditions, the double suture is articulated under the dominance of the political, which alone can *also* totalize science, as we saw when the same Stalin meddled with the legislation of genetics, linguistics or relativistic physics, in the name of the proletariat and its own Party. This situation created such a befuddled philosophical paralysis that, when in the 1960s, Louis Althusser set out to restore some of the vigor to Marxist thought, he saw no other way out than to *overthrow* the articulation of the two sutures in favor of science, and to turn philosophical Marxism into something like the epistemology of historical materialism. Nowhere is the weightiness of the sutures in philosophy during this era more visible than in the heroic attempt by which Althusser undertook to put Marxism back to the side of the suture of philosophy to science, assured as he was, that the dominance of its suture to the political condition was even more harmful. The price to pay for this transferal operation was to maintain the delegation of the political to as suspicious and dilapidated an organism as the PCF (the French Communist Party), which once more forbade that thought should seize the political for itself. After a few initial successes, the philosophical breach ran aground with the May 68 event whose naming in thought exceeded from all quarters the resources of the scientific condition, and cruelly displayed the historic lapsing of the PCF.

My conclusive thesis is the following: if philosophy is threatened by suspension, and this perhaps since Hegel, it is because it is captive of a network of sutures to its conditions, especially to its scientific and political conditions, which forbade it from configurating their *general* compossibility. It is thus correct that philosophy has indeed missed something of time, of our time, and put forth a defeated and limited image of itself.

An infallible sign by which philosophy's abrogation by some suture to one of its generic conditions can be recognized is the monotonous repetition of the statement that the 'systematic form' of philosophy is henceforth impossible. This anti-systematic axiom today is systematic. I recalled at the beginning of this book the form given to it by Lyotard, but, with the undoubted exception of Guy Lardreau and Christian Jambet, it is common to all contemporary French philosophers, and especially to those illuminated by that singular, typical constellation in which are found the Greek sophists, Nietzsche, Heidegger and Wittgenstein.

If by 'system' we understand an encyclopedic figure, itself endowed with a keystone or governed by some supreme signifier, I would gladly accept that modern desacralization forbid its deployment. Besides, has philosophy, save perhaps for Aristotle and Hegel, ever been backed by such an ambition? If by 'systematicity' we understand, as we must do, the prerequisite of a complete configuration of the four generic conditions of philosophy (which, once again, in no way demands that the *results* of these conditions be displayed or even mentioned), by means of an exposition that also exposes its expository rule, then it is of the essence of philosophy to be systematic, and no philosopher has ever doubted this, from Plato to Hegel. Moreover, this is why the refusal of 'systematicity' today goes hand in hand with the morose sentiment, which I referred to at the beginning of this text, of the 'impossibility' of philosophy itself. This is the avowal that it is not impossible at all, but *hindered* by the historic network of sutures.

I cannot grant Lyotard his definition of philosophy: a discourse in search of its own rules.[1] There are at least two universal rules, failing which one no longer has any reason to speak of philosophy. The first is that it must set the eventful naming of its conditions, and thus make possible the simultaneous and conceptually unified thinking of the matheme, the poem, political invention and the Two of love. The second is that the paradigm of the course, or of rigor, which establishes a space of thinking wherein all generic procedures find shelter and welcome, must be exhibited from within this sheltering and welcoming. This is another way of saying that philosophy is only de-sutured if it is, on its own, systematic. If *a contrario* philosophy declares the impossibility of the system, it is because it is sutured, and hands thought over to only one of its conditions.

If, in the nineteenth century and beyond, philosophy endured the dual suture to its political condition and its scientific condition, it is entirely understandable that, especially since Nietzsche, the temptation to be delivered through suturation to another condition is wielded onto it. Art was fully designated. What culminates with Heidegger is the anti-positivist and anti-Marxist effort to put philosophy in the hands of the poem. When Heidegger designates modern science, on the one hand, and the totalitarian State, on the other, as crucial effects of technology, he is in actual fact indicating the two dominant sutures from which thought will only be safe by actively undoing itself from them. The way he proposes is not that of philosophy, in his eyes realized within technology. It is the one, foreshadowed by Nietzsche, and indeed by Bergson, extended in Germany by the philosophic cult of poets, in France by the fetishism of literature (Blanchot, Derrida, Deleuze as well...), which dele-

gates the living flesh of thought to its artistic condition. In thrall in the West to science, in the East to the
political, philosophy has attempted in western Europe
to at least serve the other Master, the poem.
Philosophy's current situation is that of a harlequin
serving three masters. It may even be added that a
Levinas, in the guise of the dual talk on the Other and
its Face[2], and on Woman, considers that philosophy
could also become the valet of its fourth condition,
love.

I put forth that it is possible today, and therefore
required, to break all these contracts. The gesture I
propose is purely and simply that of philosophy, of
de-suturation. It so happens that the main stake, the
supreme difficulty, is to de-suture philosophy from its
poetic condition. Positivism and dogmatic Marxism
now constitute but ossified positions. As sutures,
they are purely institutional or academic. On the
other hand, what has given potency to the poeticizing
suture, thus to Heidegger, is far from having been
undone, indeed has never even been examined.

Who were the poets and what did they think
when philosophy was losing its own space, sutured as
it was to the matheme and to revolutionary politics?

7

⁕ ⁕

THE AGE OF POETS

In the period that opens up just after Hegel, a period in which philosophy is most often sutured either to the scientific condition or to the political one, poetry assumed certain of philosophy's functions. It is also generally accepted that this period was an exceptional one for this art. Yet, the poetry and poets we are speaking of are neither all the poetry nor all the poets, but rather those whose work is immediately recognizable as a work of thought and for whom the poem is, at the very locus where philosophy falters, a locus of language wherein a proposition about being and about time is enacted. These poets did not *decide* to take the place of philosophers; they did not write with the clarified awareness of having assumed these functions. Instead one must imagine that they were submitted to a kind of intellectual pressure, induced by the absence of free play in philosophy, the need to constitute, from within their art, that general space of reception for thought and the generic procedures that philosophy, sutured as it was, could no longer establish. If poetry was singularly designated for this labor, it is because, on the one hand, at least till Nietzsche and Heidegger, it was not among the conditions to which philosophy was sutured in a privileged way; on the other, since a distant vocation of poetry, which is the art of binding Word and experience, is to have at its chimerical horizon the ideal of Presence such that a word can found it[1]. The *rivalry* of the poet and the philosopher goes back a long way, as demonstrated by the particularly severe examination to which Plato subjects poetry and poets. The revenge on Plato, of which Nietzsche was the prophet, could not be anchored within the poem's jurisdiction. Descartes, Leibniz, Kant or Hegel might have been mathematicians, historians or physicists; if there is one thing they were not, it was poets. But since Nietzsche, all philosophers claim to be poets, they all *envy* poets, they are all wishful poets or approximate poets, or acknowledged poets, as we see with Heidegger, but also with Derrida or Lacoue-Labarthe; even Jambet or Lardreau salute the ineluctable poetic slant of the Orient's metaphysical elevations.

The fact is that there really was an *Age of Poets*, in the time of the sutured escheat of philosophers. There was a time between Hölderlin and Paul Celan when the quavering sense of what that time itself was, the most open approach to the question of Being, the space of compossibility least caught-up in brutal sutures and the most informed formulation of modern Man's experience were all unsealed and possessed by the poem. A time when the enigma of Time was caught up in the enigma of the poetic metaphor, wherein the process of unbinding was itself bound within the 'like' of the image. An entire epoch was represented in short philosophies as a consistent and especially *oriented* one. There was Progress, the sense of History, the millenarian foundation, the approach of another world and other men. But the real[ii] of this epoch was on the contrary inconsistency and disorientation. Poetry alone, or at least 'metaphysical' poetry, the most concentrated poetry, the most intellectually strained poetry, the most obscure also, designated and articulated this essential disorientation. Poetry traced in the oriented representations of History a disorienting diagonal. The scintillating dryness of these poems cut open a space—to borrow Lacoue-Labarthe's concept, stemming from Hölderlin, of "*césurer*", i.e., cutting open—within historic pathos.

The canonical representatives of the Age of Poets are the object, once philosophy attempts to suture itself to the poetic condition, of a philosophical *election*. Michel Deguy goes as far as saying (but it is true, he is a poet): "Philosophy, to prepare for poetry"[1]. In any case, to prepare the list of poets recognized by philosophy to have taken hold, at length, of its own ordinary functions.

As far as I am concerned (but I maintain that the Age of Poets is *completed*, and it is from the standpoint of this closure that my own list has been drawn up, and consequently closed), I recognize seven crucial poets, not necessarily the 'best poets'—an impossible distribution of prizes—but because they have periodized and 'scanned'[iii] the Age of Poets. These are: Hölderlin, their prophet and anticipating vigil, then all the others, who are posterior to the Paris Commune, which marked the opening of disorientation represented as oriented sense: Mallarmé, Rimbaud, Trakl, Pessoa, Mandelstam and Celan.

I do not intend to examine the historic dovetailing, the turnabouts, the founding poems, the singular operations (such as Mallarmé's Book, Rimbaud's Disordering and Pessoa's heteronyms...), so many conceptual operations whose total cannot be aligned and which constitute the Age of Poets as an age of thought. A few remarks nonetheless.

1) The fundamental line followed by our poets, which enables them to subtract themselves from the effects of philosophical sutures, is the *destitution of the category of object*. More precisely: the destitution of the category of object, and of objectivity, as necessary forms of presentation. What the poets of the Age of Poets attempt to open is an approach[iv] to being, precisely where being cannot buttress itself by way of the 'presentative' category of object. Poetry is then on essentially *disobjectifying*. This in no way signifies that sense is handed over to the subject, or the subjective. On the contrary, for what poetry is acutely conscious of is the bond[v] organized by the sutures between 'object', or objectivity, and 'subject'. This bond constitutes knowledge, or cognition. But the approach to being attempted by poetry is not of the order of cognition. It is thus diagonal to the subject/object opposition. When Rimbaud heaps sarcasm onto "subjective poetry", when Mallarmé establishes that for the poem to take place its author as subject must be absented, they mean that the *truth* of the poem emerges insofar as what it states is related to neither objectivity nor subjectivity. Because, for all the poets of the Age of Poets, if the consistency of experience is bound to objectivity, as the sutured philosophies claim by calling upon Kant, then it must be audaciously defended that *being inconsists*, as Celan summarizes admirably:

"Upon inconsistencies
to lean".

Poetry, which seeks the trace, or threshold, of Presence, denies it is possible to remain at such a threshold by conserving the theme of objectivity, and consequently a subject—the object's required correlate—cannot be the buttress for such an experience. If poetry has captured the obscurity of time in the obscure, it is because it has, whatever the diversity or even the irreconcilable dimension of its procedures, dismissed the subject-object 'objectifying' frame in which it was philosophically asserted, within the sutures, that the element of time was oriented. Poetic disorientation is first of all, by the law of a truth that makes holes in, and obliterates all cognition, that an experience, simultaneously subtracted from objectivity and subjectivity, does exist.

2) What gave potency to Heidegger's thinking was *to have crossed the strictly philosophical critique of objectivity with its poetic destitution.* His stroke of genius—apart from the fact that it is merely just a mode of suturation, this time to the poetic condition—was:

— to have grasped, particularly through his examination of Kant, that what separated "fundamental ontology" from the doctrine of cognition was the maintenance, in the latter, of the category of object, the guideline and absolute limit of the Kantian critique;

— to have avoided, for all that, falling into subjectivism or into a radical philosophy of consciousness, a path ultimately followed by Husserl, but on the contrary to have pronounced the deconstruction of the theme of the subject, which he considered as the last avatar of metaphysics and the correlative constraint of objectivity;

— to have remained steadfast in the capital distinction between knowledge and truth, or between cognition and thought, a distinction that is the latent foundation of the poetic venture;

— to have thus reached the point at which it is possible to *hand philosophy over to poetry*. This suture seems like a guarantee of strength, for *it is true* that there was an Age of Poets. The existence of the poets gave to Heidegger's thinking, something without which it would have been aporetic and hopeless, a ground of historicity, actuality, apt to confer to it— once the mirage of a political historicity had been concretized and dissolved in the Nazi horror—what was to be its unique, real occurrence.

Until today, Heidegger's thinking has owed its persuasive power to having been the only one to pick up what was at stake in the poem, namely the destitution of object fetishism, the opposition of truth and knowledge and lastly the essential disorientation of our epoch.

For this reason, the fundamental criticism of Heidegger can only be the following one: the Age of Poets is completed, it is *also* necessary to de-suture philosophy from its poetic condition. Which means that it is no longer required today that disobjectivation and disorientation be stated in the poetic metaphor. Disorientation can be *conceptualized*.

3) There is however in the Heideggerian appraisal of the Age of Poets a point of falsification. Heidegger proceeds as if the poetic statement[vi] identified the destitution of objectivity and the destitution of science. In risking the Open from the very heart of technological distress, the poem would summon forth "modern science", would expose it, in the category of the objectivation of the world and of the subject as annihilating will. Heidegger 'constructs'[vii] the antinomy of the matheme and the poem *in such a way as to make it coincide with the opposition of knowledge and truth, or the subject/object couple and Being*. Now, this 'mon-

tage' cannot be read in the poetry of the Age of Poets. The authentic relation of poets to mathematics is of a completely different nature. It takes the form of a relation of raveled rivalry, of heterogeneous communities *occupying the same point*. The 'algebraic' will of Mallarmean poetry is evident and when he writes "you mathematicians expired" it is only to point out that in the specific locus where the 'conspiration'[viii] of chance and infinity actively plays itself out, poetry *sublates* the matheme. When Rimbaud notes—and so passing a particularly profound sentence on the literal essence of science—: "Weak-minded people, beginning to *think about* the first letter of the alphabet, would rush into madness"[2], he inscribes with the same stroke the passion of the matheme on the side of salvational disorders, for what is mathematics ultimately other than the decision to use letters to *think*? Lautréamont, the dignified heir to Plato, Spinoza and Kant, considers that mathematics saved him, and it did so at the specific point of the destitution of the subject-object or Man-world couple: "Oh rigorous mathematics, I have not forgotten you since your wise lessons, sweeter than honey, filtered into my heart like a refreshing wave.... Without you, in my struggle against man, I would perhaps have been defeated".[3]

And when Pessoa writes: "Newton's binomial theory is as beautiful as the Venus de Milo/The fact is, precious few persons care"[4], he makes us think: rather than opposing the truth of the poem to the latent nihilism of the matheme, the imperative is to have this identity of beauty finally perceived by the whole world, not just by the "precious few".

Poetry, thus more profound than its philosopher servant, has been altogether aware of a *sharing of thinking* with mathematics, since it has blindly perceived that the matheme too, in its pure, literal offering, in its empty suture to every multiple-presentation, was questioning and dismissing the prevalence of objectivity. Poets have, it is true, known better than mathematicians themselves that there was no such thing as a mathematical *object*.

Every suture is an exaggeration, for as I have repeated with Heidegger, philosophy compounds problems. Sutured to one of its conditions, philosophy lends it virtues imperceptible from within the exercise of this condition. By isolating the poem as the unique figure of thought and risk, as an instance of distress and salvation partaking of destiny; by going so far as to consider, following René Char, a "power of poets and thinkers"[5], Heidegger exceeded the poetic jurisdiction that, short of "taking the pose", which is alas Char's case more often than his own, does not legislate such uniqueness and in particular deals with the matheme—and also with the political and love—from an altogether other angle. He has done no more with respect to the poem than those—I was among them—that philosophically absolutized the political from within the Marxist suture, well beyond what *real* politics was able to state about itself. No more than what in the guise of fabulous promises Positivist philosophers extracted from a science unable to give any, and for which a promise, of any kind, is altogether foreign.

4) The central operation from which we may receive and consider a poet from the Age of Poets is his 'method' of disobjectivation. Hence the procedure, most often very complex, that he implements to produce truths for want of knowledge, to state the disorientation in the metaphorical movement of a destitution of the subject-object couple. These procedures differentiate the poets, and periodize the Age of Poets. They are

mainly of two types: the implementing of a lack or
that of an excess. The object is either subtracted,
withdrawn from Presence by its own self-dissolution
(Mallarmé's method) or extracted from its domain of
apparition, unraveled by its solitary exception and
from then on rendered substitutable to every other
one (Rimbaud's method). The poem orders lack or disorders presentation.[ix] The subject is simultaneously
terminated either by being absented (Mallarmé) or by
actual pluralization (Pessoa, Rimbaud: "With some
men, I often talked out loud with a moment from one
of their other lives—that's how I happened to love a
pig."[6] Nothing is better than the inventory of these
procedures to indicate the extent to which these
poems are closely related, in fact provisionally substituted, to the 'construct' of the space of thinking which
defines philosophy.

5) Paul Celan's work states, at the terminal edge,
and from within poetry, the end of the Age of Poets.
Celan completes Heidegger.

8

✳ ✳

EVENTS

That it be today possible, and so necessary to de-suture philosophy and proclaim its renaissance; that, following the long suspension entailed by the successive and ruinous privileges of the scientific condition (positivisms), the political condition (marxisms) and the poetic condition (from Nietzsche till today), the imperative is once again to configurate the four conditions starting from an entirely recast doctrine of truth; that, at odds with the repeated announcements of the 'end of philosophy', the 'end of metaphysics', the 'crisis of reason', the 'deconstruction of the subject', the task is to *resume* the thread of modern reason, to take *one more step* in the lineage of the 'Cartesian meditation': this would only amount to arbitrary willfulness if what had grounded its sense did not have the status of crucial events having occurred, albeit in accordance with still suspended or precarious naming, in the register of each of the four conditions. These are the events of the matheme, the poem, thinking on love and inventive politics that prescribe the return of philosophy, in their aptitude to set up an intellectual place of shelter and collection for that which, of these events, is henceforth namable.

In the order of the matheme, the route leading from Cantor to Paul Cohen constitutes this event.[1] It founds the central paradox of the theory of the multiple, fully and demonstratively articulating for the first time in a discernible concept what is an indiscernible multiplicity. It *resolves* conversely to the way Leibniz proposed, the question of knowing whether a rational thinking of being *qua* being abides by the sovereignty of language. We know today it is not the case, and that, on the contrary, it is only by taking into account the existence of any unnamable, 'generic' multiplicities whatever, delimited by no properties of language, that we may have the chance to approach the truth of the being of a given multiple. If truth makes a hole in knowledge, if there is hence no knowledge of truth, but only a *production* of truths, it is because, mathematically thought in its being—thus as a pure multiplicity—a truth is generic, subtracted from all exact designations, in excess with regard to what these designations afford to discern. The price to pay for this certainty is that the *quantity* of a multiple tolerates an indeterminacy, a kind of disjunctive rift that constitutes the whole of the real of being itself: it is strictly *impossible* to think the quantitative relation between the 'number' of members of an infinite multiplicity and the number of its parts. This relation has the form only of a *wandering excess*: it is known that the parts are more numerous than the members (Cantor's Theorem), but no measure of this 'more' can be established.

It is moreover at this real point—wandering excess in the quantitative infinite—that the great *orientations in thought* are established. *Nominalist* thought refuses this result and admits only namable multiplicities into existence. It is prior to the event of the matheme I am speaking about. It is thus conservative thinking. *Transcendent* thought believes that the determination of a multiple-point situated over and above ordinary measures will regulate and fix, 'from above', the wandering of the excess. It is thinking that tolerates the indiscernible but as a transitory effect of an ignorance relative to some 'supreme' multiple. It therefore does not ratify excess and wandering as laws of being. It hopes for a complete language while admitting that we do not yet dispose of one. It is prophetic thinking. Finally, *generic* thought takes on the indiscernible as the type of being of every truth, and holds the wandering of the excess to be the real of being, the being of being. Since the upshot of this is that every truth is an infinite production suspended to an event, irreducible to all established knowledge and determined only by the *activity* of those faithful to this event, it can be said that generic thinking is, in the widest sense of the term, militant thinking. If we must take the risk here of a *name* for the event of the matheme, whose philosophic contemporaries we are, we shall concur that this event is that of an indiscernible or generic multiplicity, as the being-in-truth of the pure multiple (therefore: as the truth of being *qua* being).

In the order of love, of the thinking of what it conveys with respect to truths, the work of Jacques Lacan constitutes an event. We need not enter here into the supplementary question of the status of psychoanalysis, previously couched in reference to the positivist suture in the form of 'Is psychoanalysis a science?', which I shall rather state in the following way: 'Is psychoanalysis a generic procedure? Does it belong to the conditions of philosophy?' Let us simply note the following: given that from Plato till Freud and Lacan, philosophy has only known four generic procedures, it would be considerable, and would somewhat justify the frequent arrogance of followers of psychoanalysis, should psychoanalysis force philosophy to deal with a fifth one. This would in fact be a revolution in thought, a completely new epoch of the configurating activities of philosophy. But supposing psychoanalysis is but an apparatus of opinion leaning on institutional practices, the upshot would only be that Freud and Lacan are in reality philosophers, great thinkers who, *regarding* this apparatus of opinion, have contributed to putting into concepts the general space wherein the generic procedures of the time come to find the shelter and welcome of their compossibility. In any case, they will have had the immense merit of maintaining and founding the category of the subject again in times when philosophy, diversely sutured, abdicated on this point. They will have, in their way, pursued the 'Cartesian meditation', and it is by no means a coincidence that Lacan, from the very beginning of his essential work, issued the call for a "return to Descartes". Perhaps they were only able to accomplish this by rebutting the status of the philosopher, indeed in drawing their inspiration, as did Lacan, from anti-philosophy. Freud and Lacan's situation of thinking was undoubtedly to *accompany*, as its inversion, the desubjectifying operation of the Age of Poets.

It may seem out of the ordinary to make of Lacan a theoretician of love, and not of the subject or of desire. The fact is that, here, I am examining his thinking from the strict point of view of the conditions of philosophy. It is quite possible (but the number and complexity of texts he devotes to it are nonetheless symptomatic) that love is not a central concept in Lacan's explicit work. It is however from the angle of the innovations in thinking which deal with it, that his undertaking is an event and a condition for the renaissance of philosophy. I moreover know of no theory of love having been as profound as his since Plato's, the Plato of the *Symposium* that Lacan dialogues with over and over again. When Lacan writes: "It is love that accosts being as such in the encounter"[2], the specifically ontological function he assigns to love clearly shows the kind of insertion he is conscious of implementing in the configurations of philosophy with respect to theories of love.

Love is that from which the Two is thought, by the slitting of the dominance of the One, whose image love nonetheless endures. We know that Lacan proceeds to a kind of logical deduction of the Two of the sexes, of the woman "share" and the man "share" of a subject, a partition combining negation and—universal and existential—quantifiers to define a woman as "not-all"[3], and the masculine pole as a vector of the All or the Whole thus broken off. Love is the actuality of this paradoxical Two, which in itself is in the element of the non-relation, of the un-bound.[1] It is the "access" of the Two as such. Originated in the event of an encounter (the 'sudden' on which Plato had already strongly insisted), love weaves infinite or incompletable experience of that which of this Two already constitutes an irremediable excess with respect to the law of the One. I shall say in my language that love makes a truth about sexuation come forth as a nameless or generic multiplicity, a truth obviously subtracted from knowledge, especially from the knowledge of those who love each other. Love is the production, with fidelity to the encounter-event, of a truth about the Two.

Lacan is event-making for philosophy since he organizes all kinds of subtleties about the Two, about the image of the One in the un-bound of the Two, and arranges the generic paradoxes of love within it. Moreover, nourished by his experience, he knows just as well how to state, for example, in reference or comparison to courtly love, the contemporary state of the question of love. Not only does he propose a concept, articulated according to the quibbling of difference and its brisk procedure, but he also proposes an analysis of conjuncture. This is why the anti-philosopher Lacan is a condition of the renaissance of philosophy. A philosophy is possible today, only if it is compossible with Lacan.

In the order of the political, the event is concentrated in the historic sequence which stretches from about 1965 to 1980, and which has seen the succession of what Sylvain Lazarus calls "obscure events", that is: obscure from the point of view of politics.[4] These include: May 68 and its aftermath, the Chinese Cultural Revolution, the Iranian Revolution, the working class and national movement in Poland ('Solidarity'). This is not the place to say whether these events, in terms of pure facts, were favorable or ill-fated, victorious or vanquished. What is sure is that we are *in suspension of their naming as political events.* Undoubtedly with the exception of the Polish movement, these politico-historic instances are all the more opaque that they gave themselves a representation of themselves, in the consciousness of their actors, in frameworks of thinking whose outdated character they pronounced at the same time. It is thus that May 68 or the Cultural Revolution made commonly reference to Marxist-Leninism, about which it soon appeared that the ruin—as a system of political representation—was in actual fact inscribed in the very nature of the events. What was taking place, although thought within this system, was not therein thinkable. In the same way, the Iranian

Revolution was inscribed in often archaistic Islamic preaching, whereas the core of popular conviction and its symbolization exceeded this preaching from all quarters. Nothing has better attested to the fact that an event is supernumerary, not only with respect to its site but also to the language available to it, than this discord between the opacity of the intervention and the vain transparency of representations. The upshot of this discord is that the events in question *are not yet named*, or rather that the work of their naming (what I call the *intervention* on the event) is not yet complete, far from it. Today, politics is, among other things, the capacity to faithfully stabilize this naming, and for the long haul.

Philosophy is under the condition of the political to the exact extent that what it sets as conceptual space proves to be homogenous to this stabilization, whose own process is strictly political. It can be seen how May 68, Poland, etc., participate in the desuturing of philosophy: what is at stake here as to the political is certainly not *transitive* to philosophy, as 'dialectical materialism' claimed to be to Stalinian politics. It is on the contrary the excessive dimension of the event and the task it prescribes *to the political* which condition philosophy, because it has the duty to establish that the politically *invented* acts of naming the event are compossible with what simultaneously (that is: for our epoch) creates a rupture in the order of the matheme, the poem and love. Philosophy is once again possible precisely because it does not have to legislate on History or on the political, but only to think the contemporary re-opening of the possibility of the political, stemming from obscure events.

In the order of the poem, the event is Paul Celan's work, in and of itself as well as through what it holds from the entire Age of Poets at its ultimate edge. It is symptomatic that it is in reference to Celan's poems that ventures of thinking as diverse as those of Derrida's, Gadamer's or Lacoue-Labarthe's pronounce the ineluctable suture of philosophy to its poetic condition. The sense I grant to these poems (but already, in a certain way, to those of Pessoa and Mandelstam) is exactly the inverse. In them I read, as poetically stated, the avowal that poetry no longer suffices to itself; that it *requests* to be relieved of the burden of the suture; that it hopes for a philosophy relieved of the crushing authority of the poem. Lacoue-Labarthe had the diverted intuition of this request when he deciphered with Celan an "interruption of art". The interruption in my view is not of poetry, but of the poetry *philosophy has handed itself over to*. Celan's drama is to have had to confront sense in the non-sense of the epoch, its disorientation, with nothing but the solitary resource of the poem. When in *Anabasis* he evokes the ascent ("upward and back") toward "the tent-word:/ Together"[5], it is to the outer-poem he aspires, to the sharing of thinking less plunged into metaphoric uniqueness. The imperative poetry bequeaths to us, the event whose name it enjoins us to find *elsewhere*, is the poetic call to the reconstitution of a testament of the conceptual disposition of our time; it is the formulation in the poem of the end of the Age of Poets, which we too often forget brought glory but also torment and solitude to its poets, a solitude compounded, and not diminished, by the philosophies sutured within it.

Everything hinges, it is quite true, on the sense we give to the encounter between Celan and Heidegger, a quasi-mythical episode of our epoch. Lacoue-Labarthe's argument is that the Jewish poet survivor could not, what? Tolerate? Support? In any case, overlook the fact that the poets' philosopher kept in Celan's presence—and in every presence—the most complete silence about the Extermination. I do not for a second doubt this to be the case. But there is also the fact, and necessarily so, that to go see the philosopher was to experience what the ascent "upward and back" toward the sense of the epoch could expect from him, in the element of the outer-poem. Yet, this philosopher referred to the poem, precisely in such a way as to make the poet feel more alone in his presence than ever before. It has to be seen that Heidegger's question "what are poets for?", can become for the poet "what are philosophers for?", and that if the answer to this question is "for there to be poets", the solitude of the poet is redoubled. Celan's work makes an event of this solitude by asking, from the position of the poem, that an end be put to it.

These two meanings of the encounter moreover are not contradictory. How could Heidegger break the poem's mirror—which Celan's poetry does in its own way—he who did not believe it possible to elucidate, in the order of political conditions, his own National Socialist involvement? This silence, aside from most deeply offending the Jewish poet, was also an irreme-diable philosophic deficiency because it brought to its peak, and to the point of the intolerable, the reductive and nihilating effects of the suture. Celan could expe-rience here what the philosophical fetishism of the poem ultimately produced. The most profound sense of his poetic work is to deliver us from this fetishism, to free the poem from its speculative parasites, to restore it to the fraternity of its time, where it will thereafter have to dwell side by side in thought with the matheme, love and political invention. The event is that, in hopelessness and anxiety, Celan the poet detects within poetry the pass of this restitution.

Such are the events that, in each of the generic procedures, today condition philosophy. Our duty is to produce a conceptual configuration liable to greet them, as little named, indeed located, as they may still be. How are Paul Cohen's generic, Lacan's theory of love, the political fidelity to May 68 and to Poland, and Celan's poetic call to the outer-poem simultaneously possible for thought? It is not in the least a question of totalizing them: these events are heterogeneous and cannot be aligned. It is a question of producing the concepts and rules of thinking, perhaps farthest off from any explicit mention of these names and acts, perhaps very close to them, it all depends. But in such a way that through these concepts and rules, our time will be represented as the time in which *this event of thought has taken place*. An event never having taken place before and which is henceforth the shared lot of everyone, whether they know it or not, since a philosophy has constituted for everyone the common shelter of this "having-taken-place".

9

✳ ✳

QUESTIONS

In its *content*, the gesture of recomposition of philosophy I propose is widely dictated by the singularity of the events which have affected the four generic procedures (Cantor-Gödel-Cohen for the matheme, Lacan for the concept of love, Pessoa-Mandelstam-Celan for the poem, the sequence of obscure events between 1965 and 1980, for political invention). The great conceptual questions induced by the suspension of these occurrences of thought, and which must be philosophically projected in a unique space (where thoughts of our time will be thought), are extricated quite clearly once the eventful locating has been accomplished. Moreover, even though they deny the right of philosophy to exist and polemicize against systematicity, our philosophers, Heideggerians, modern sophists, metaphysical Lacanians, doctrinaires of the poem and sectarians of proliferating multiplicities, all work on these questions: one cannot subtract oneself so easily from the imperative, even misunderstood, of the conditions, for what founds the imperative *has taken place.*

A first of these questions is that of the Two, over and above its ordinary formulation, that is, dialectics. I have shown that it buttressed the whole analytics of love. But it is quite clear that it is at the heart of political innovation in the form of the place that strife must henceforth occupy in it. Classical Marxism was a strong dualism: the proletariat against the bourgeoisie. It made antagonism the key to any representation of the political. 'Class struggle' and 'revolution', then–in the Statist vision of things—'dictatorship of the proletariat', laid the framework for the field of reflecting on practices. The political was only thinkable insofar as the movement of History was structured by an essential Two, founded in the real of economics and exploitation. The political 'concentrated the economy', which means it organized the strategy of the Two around the power of the State. It had as an ultimate aim the destruction of the political machinery of the adversary. It substituted a global clash to the dispersed and more or less peaceful clashes which set, on the social terrain, the exploited against the exploiters, each class being projected into a political organism representing it, a political party of class. Ultimately, only violence (insurrection or prolonged popular war) could sever the conflict. But precisely, what the obscure events of the 1960s and 1970s have placed on the agenda of the day, is the decline, the historic untimeliness of this potent conception. What is being sought after today is a thinking of the political which, while dealing with strife, having the structural Two in its field of intervention, does not have this Two as an objective essence. Or rather, to the objectivist doctrine of the Two (classes are transitive to the process of production), the political innovation under way attempts to oppose a vision of the Two 'in terms of historicity', which means that the real

Two is an eventful *production*, a political production, and not an objective or 'scientific' presupposition. Today, we must proceed to a *reversal* of the question of the Two: as the classic example of the concept in terms of objectivity (class struggle, or the duality of the sexes, or Good and Evil...), the Two will become what chance production, fastened to an event, is pinned onto. The Two, and not as in the past the One, is what befalls; the Two is post-eventful. The One (unity of class, amorous fusion, Salvation...) was bestowed onto man as his difficulty and his task. We shall rather consider that nothing is more difficult than the Two, nothing is more simultaneously subjected to chance and to faithful labor. Man's highest duty is to jointly produce the Two and the thinking of the Two, *the exercise* of the Two.

The second question is that of the object and objectivity. I have shown that the decisive function of the poets of the Age of Poets was to establish that access to being and truth presupposed the destitution of the category of object as an organic form of presentation. The object may well be a category of knowledge, it still hinders the post-eventful production of truths. Poetic disobjectivation, the condition of an opening to our epoch as a disoriented one, authorizes the following philosophical statement in its radical nudity: every truth is *without an object*.

The fundamental problem is then the following one: does the destitution of the category of object entail the destitution of the category of subject? This is without any doubt the visible effect of most of the poems of the Age of Poets. I have noted the pluralization, the dissemination of the subject in Rimbaud and its being absented in Mallarmé. The subject of Trakl's poetry only occupies the locus of Death. Sutured as he is to poets, it is only in vain that Heidegger says it is impossible to think the contemporary site of Man from the categories of subject and object. *A contrario*, Lacan was the guardian of the subject only insofar as he *also* took up and elaborated the category of object again. In terms of cause of desire, the Lacanian object (very close in actual fact, by its unsymbolizable and punctual feature, to Kant's "the transcendental object = x") is the determination of the subject *in its being*, which Lacan makes explicit in the following way: "The subject that believes it can have access to itself by designating itself in the statement is nothing else but such an object."[1]

One can summarize the situation from the logic of sutures, such that it has presided to this day over the unbeing[ii] of contemporary philosophy. Philosophies sutured to their scientific condition attach the greatest importance to the category of object, and objectivity is their acknowledged norm. Philosophies sutured to the political condition, that is, the variants of the 'old Marxism', either posit that a subject 'emerges' from objectivity (the passage of the 'class-in-itself' to the 'class-for-itself', generally by way of the virtue of the Party). Or else, more consequently, they destitute the subject to the benefit of objectivity (for Althusser, the matter of truth is related to the subjectless procedure), and paradoxically join Heidegger by making the subject a simple operator of bourgeois ideology (for Heidegger, "subject" is a secondary elaboration of the reign of technology, but we can see eye to eye if this reign is in fact also the bourgeoisie's). For philosophies sutured to the poem, or more broadly to literature, to art even, thought does without the object as well as the subject. For Lacanians finally, there are admissible concepts of both. Everyone concurs on a single point, which is so general an axiom of philosophic modernity that I can but rally to it: there is in any case no question of defining truth as a "likening^{iii} of the subject and the object". Everyone diverges when it comes to actually laying out the critique of likeness, since they do not agree on the status of the terms (subject and object) between which it operates.

It should be noticed that this typology leaves a locus void: a locus of thinking which would maintain the category of subject, but would grant the poets the destitution of the object. The task of such thinking is to produce a concept of the subject such that it is supported by no mention of the object, a subject, if I might say, *without a vis-a-vis*. This locus has a bad reputation, for it evokes Bishop Berkeley's absolute idealism. As you have realized, it is, yet, to the task of occupying it that I am devoted. I maintain the problem of the *subject without object* as central as regards a possible renaissance of philosophy, just as disobjectivation, disjoining truth from knowledge, founded the Age of Poets, hence the decisive critique of the positivist and marxian sutures. Moreover, I maintain that one sole concept, the generic procedure, subsumes the disobjectivation of truth and of the subject, making the subject appear as a simple finite fragment of a post-eventful truth without object. It is only on the route of the objectless subject that we can simultaneously re-open the 'Cartesian meditation' and remain faithful to the assets of the Age of Poets, a specifically philosophic fidelity, thus a desutured one. It is, for all that, to such a movement of thought, I am convinced of it, that Paul Celan's poetry convened us, and particularly the mysterious injunction, combining the idea that the approach to being is not the disclosed and royal route of objectivity, and that of the subtractive prevalence of marks, or the inscription, on the misleading expanse of sensible offering:

A sense also looms
along the narrowest trail

fractured by
the most mortal of our
erected markings

The third question is that of the indiscernible.
Today, the sovereignty of language is a general dogma,
although between the "exact language" which the posi-
tivists dream of, and the Heideggerians' "poetic statement", there is more than one misunderstanding
about the essence of language. Just as an abyss separates Foucault's integral nominalism from Lacan's
doctrine of the symbolic. What everyone nonetheless
agrees on, lodged as they are in what Lyotard calls the
"Great Linguistic Turn" of Western philosophy, is that
on the selvages of language and of being, there is
nothing, and that either a possible 'gathering of being'
in language does exist or what is is only such from
being named, or being as such is subtracted from language, something which has never meant anything
else than handing it over to *another language*, be it
that of the poet, of the Unconscious or of God.

I have already indicated that, as far as this point
is concerned, only the matheme guides us. Contemporary conviction is the same as Leibniz's: there can
be no indiscernibles for thought, if what is meant by
'indiscernible' is an explicit *concept* of what is subtracted from language. Of what is subtracted from language, there can be no concept, no thought. This is
the reason why Lacan's unsymbolizable real is "horror". Notwithstanding, to what befalls as it befalls,
Lyotard believes it necessary to give the name of "sentence"[iv]. What is not namable—better keep it at arm's
length from thought. Of Leibniz's "Principle of the

Indiscernibles", Wittgenstein, at the end of the *Tractatus*, gave the version which is now the consensus: "Whereof one cannot speak, thereof one must be silent."[2]

Now, we know that ever since the event in the matheme constituted by Paul Cohen's operators, it is precisely possible to produce a concept of the indiscernible and to establish under certain conditions the existence of multiplicities that fall within this concept: 'generic' multiplicities. It is thus quite simply false that whereof one cannot speak (in the sense of 'there is nothing to say about it that specifies it and grants it separating properties'), thereof one must be silent. It must on the contrary be named. It must be discerned as indiscernible. We are no longer held, if we accept to be within the effects of the mathematical condition, to choose between the namable and the unthinkable. We are no longer suspended between something whereof there is an elucidation within language, and something whereof there is but an ineffable, indeed unbearable 'experience', unraveling the mind. For the indiscernible, even though it breaks down the separating powers of language, is nonetheless proposed to the concept, which can demonstratively pass legislation on its existence.

It is, from this point, possible to return to the object and the Two, and to show the profound bond existing between our three problems. If truth has no need of the category of object, it is precisely because it is always, as the result of an infinite procedure, an indiscernible multiple. If the Two is foreign to any objective foundation of the political or of love, it is because these procedures aim at *indiscerning* existential or popular subsets, and not at hurling them 'against' what dominates their situation. It is because love *supplements* a life, rather than binds one to another. It is because politics, from its founding event, tends to delimit the undelimitable, to make people exist as a multiple, whose established language can neither grasp the community nor its interest. If, finally, the Two is a production, and not a state, it is because what it distinguishes step by step of the situation in which the One reigns, is not 'an other One', but the immanent figure of what *has not been counted.*

Today philosophy must knot together the destitution of the object, the reversal of the instance of the Two and the thinking of the indiscernible. It must withdraw from the form of objectivity *to the benefit of the sole subject,* maintain the Two as the fortuitous and tenacious descendant of the event, and identify Truth with the nondescript, the nameless, the generic. To knot these three prescriptions together supposes a complex space of thinking whose central concept is that of the objectless subject, itself the consequence of genericity as the faithful becoming, in being itself, of an event supplementing it. Such a space, if we manage to organize it, will greet the contemporary figure of the four conditions of philosophy.

As for its *form,* the philosophical gesture I propose is Platonic.

10

** **

PLATONIC GESTURE

Recognizing the end of the Age of Poets, sum-
moning contemporary forms of the matheme as the
vector of ontology, thinking love from the point of view
of its truth–function, inscribing the directions of a
beginning of the political: these four gestures are
Platonic. Plato must also keep the poets, innocent
accomplices to sophistry, out of the project of philosophical foundation, incorporate the mathematical
processing of the problem of irrational numbers into
his vision of the 'logos', do justice to the suddenness
of love in the ascension toward the Beautiful and the
Forms, and think the twilight of the democratic Polis.
To which the following must be added: just as Plato
has the professionals of sophistry, at once bullheaded
and bearers of modernity, as his interlocutors, so also
does the attempt to radicalize the rupture with classical categories of thought today define what is reasonable to call a 'Great Sophistry', linked essentially to
Wittgenstein. The decisive importance of language
and its variability in heterogeneous games, doubt as
to the pertinence of the concept of truth, rhetorical
proximity to the effects of art, pragmatic and open

politics: so many features common to the Greek
sophists and to any number of contemporary orientations, which explain why studies and references
devoted to Gorgias or Protagoras have recently been
multiplied. We too are confronted by the obligation of
a critique of sophistic rigor, with due respect for all
the teachings it entails about the epoch. The young
Plato knew he had to go beyond the subtle wrangling
of sophistry as well as be educated by it about the
essence of the questions of his time. The same holds
true for us. That the transition under way between
the age of sutures and the age of philosophy's new
beginning marks the reign of the sophists is altogether natural. Great Modern Sophistry, linguistic,
æstheticizing and democratic, exercises its dissolving
function, examines impasses and draws the picture of
what is contemporary to us. It is just as essential for
us as the libertine was to Blaise Pascal: it *alerts* us to
the singularities of the time.

An anti-sophistic configuration of the matheme
(as inaugural), the poem (as dismissed), the political
(as founded again) and love (as thought)—the philosophical gesture I propose is a Platonic one. The century, till now, has been anti-Platonic. I do not know of
a theme more widespread in the most varied and
divided philosophic schools than anti-Platonism.
Under the heading 'Plato' in the philosophy dictionary
commissioned by Stalin, we could read "ideologue of
the slave owners", which was short and blunt. But
Sartrian existentialism in its polemic against essences
had Plato as its target. But Heidegger dates the beginning of oblivion from the "Platonic Turning", whatever
his respect may be for what there still is of Greek in
the luminous cutting-up of the Form. But contemporary philosophy of language takes the side of the
sophists against Plato. But the thinking of Human

Rights traces the totalitarian temptation back to Plato—this is notably Popper's inspiration. But Lacoue-Labarthe seeks to ferret out in the ambiguous relation of Plato to mimesis, the origin of the destiny of the political in the West. There is no end to enumerating all the anti-Platonic sequences, all the grievances, all the deconstructions in which Plato is at stake.

The great 'inventor' of contemporary anti-Platonism, at the dawn of the suture of philosophy to the poem, and because Platonism was the main ban on such a suture, was Nietzsche. The diagnosis Nietzsche established in the preface to *Beyond Good and Evil* is well known: "Indeed, as a physician one might ask: 'How could the most beautiful growth of antiquity, Plato, contract such a disease ?'"[1] Plato is the name of the spiritual disease of the West. Christianity itself is nothing but a "Platonism for the use of 'the people'". But what fills Nietzsche with elation, what finally gives free reign to "free spirits", is that the West is starting its convalescence: "Europe is breathing freely again after this nightmare." In actual fact, the superseding of Platonism is under way, and this current superseding gives forth an energy of thinking that is without precedent: "the fight against Plato... has created a magnificent tension of the spirit in Europe the likes of which had never yet existed on earth." The "free, very free spirits", the "good Europeans", hold in their hands the bow thus bent and possess the "arrow, the task and—who knows?—the *goal.*" We know that it would soon appear that this "goal" was—once the bloody, unnamable lie of its political assumption had dissipated—the pure and simple delivery of thought to the poem. Nietzsche's polemic against the "Plato-disease", the application point of European therapy, pertains to the concept of truth. The radical axiom from which "free spirits" can ensure Platonism's wake, a wake that is the wakefulness of thought as well as its awakening, lies in the dismissal of truth: "The falseness of a judgment is for us not necessarily an objection to a judgment." Nietzsche ushers in a century given over to antagonism and to potency through this complete eradication of the reference to truth, held as the major symptom of the Plato-disease. To be cured of Platonism is first and foremost to be cured of truth. And this cure would not be complete were it not itself accompanied by a resolute hatred of the matheme, held as a carapace in which the diseased weakness of the Platonist nests: "Or consider the hocus-pocus of mathematical form with which Spinoza clad his philosophy...in mail and mask, to strike terror at the very outset into the heart of any assailant...how much personal timidity and vulnerability this masquerade of a sick hermit betrays!" Philosophy through aphorisms and fragments, poems and enigmas, metaphors and maxims—the whole Nietzschean style, which has had so many echoes in contemporary thought, roots itself in the dual exigencies of the destitution of truth and the dismissal of the matheme. An anti-Platonist till the end, Nietzsche subjects the matheme to the plight Plato reserves for the poem, that of a suspect weakness, a disease of thought, a "masquerade".

There is no doubt as to Nietzsche's enduring victory. It is true that the century has "been cured" of Platonism, and that, in its most vigorous thinking, it has been sutured to the poem, abandoning the matheme to the quibbling of the positivist suture. The *a contrario* proof is given to us by the following: the only great openly Platonic as well as modern thinking was Albert Lautman's, in the 1930s. This thinking is structured right through by mathematics. For a long time it was buried and unrecognized after the Nazis had interrupted its course by murdering Lautman. Today it is the only fulcrum we can discover in almost a hundred years for the Platonic proposal the current moment requires of us, if we put aside the 'Platonizing' spontaneity of many mathematicians, in particular Gödel and Cohen, and of course the Lacanian doctrine of truth. Everything happened as though the Nietzschean utterance had sealed, in the guise of the suture to the poem, the jointly anti-matheme and anti-truth destiny of a century. Today the Nietzschean diagnosis must be toppled. The century and Europe must imperatively be cured of anti-Platonism. Philosophy shall only exist insofar as it proposes, to match the needs of our times, a new step in the history of the category of truth. It is truth which is a new idea in Europe today. And as with Plato, as with Lautman, the novelty of this idea is illuminated in the frequenting of mathematics.

11

* *

GENERIC

What a modern philosopher retains of Great Sophistry is the following point: Being is essentially multiple. Plato had already, in the *Theatetus*, pointed out that the ontology underlying the sophistic proposal is coherent with the multiple mobility of being and, rightly or wrongly, he passed this ontology off as Heraclitus'. But Plato reserved the rights to the One. Our situation is more complex for we have to recognize, under guidance of the school of Great Modern Sophistry, after many grueling avatars, that our century will have been the century of protest against the One. We cannot revoke the without-being of the One nor the limitless authority of the multiple. God is truly dead, as are all the categories that used to depend on it in the order of the thinking of being. The pass that is ours is a *Platonism of the multiple.*

Plato thought he could ruin the linguistic and rhetorical variance of sophistry from the aporia of an ontology of the multiple. To be sure, we in turn encounter this connection between the flexible availability of language (Wittgenstein's theory of language games) and the multiple-form of presentation (Deleuze's subtle descriptive investigations). But the weak point has changed places: we must *take on* the multiple and rather mark the radical limits of what language can constitute. Whence the crucial nature of the question of the indiscernible.

The main difficulty is tied to the category of truth. If being is multiple, how can this category be saved, a salvation that is the true center of gravity of every Platonic gesture? For there to be a truth, does the One of a multiplicity not have to be pronounced first, and is it not regarding this One that a truth judgment is possible? In addition, if being is multiple, a truth must also be multiple unless it has no being. But how can a truth be conceived as multiple in its being? Holding steady to the multiple, Great Modern Sophistry renounces the category of truth just as the 'relativists' of Greek sophistry already had. Here again, Nietzsche inaugurates the trial of truth in the name of the multiple potency of life. As we are unable to subtract ourselves from the jurisdiction of this potency on the thinking of being, we are forced to propose a doctrine of truth compatible with the irreducible multiplicity of being *qua* being. A truth can only be the singular production of a multiple. The whole point is that this multiple will be subtracted from the authority of language. It will be indiscernible, or rather: it *will have been* indiscernible.

The central category here is *generic* multiplicity. It founds the Platonism of the multiple by letting us think a truth as both a multiple-result of a singular procedure, and as a hole, or subtraction, in the field of the namable. It makes it possible to take on an ontology of the pure multiple without renouncing truth and without having to recognize the constituting nature of language variation. It is, in addition, the framework of a thinking space wherein the four conditions of philosophy can be gathered and located as compossible. The poem, the matheme, inventive politics and love in their contemporary state are in fact nothing but the *actual* regimes of production, in multiple situations, of generic multiples making truth of these situations.

The concept of the generic multiple was first produced in the field of mathematical activity. It was in fact proposed by Paul Cohen at the beginning of the sixties to resolve very technical problems that had been left in abeyance for nearly a century concerning the 'power', or pure quantity of certain infinite multiplicities. It can be said that the concept of the generic multiple closed the first stage of the ontological theory that, since Cantor, goes by the name of 'Set Theory'. In *L'Etre et l'Evénement*, I completely unfolded the dialectic between the mathematical edification of the theory of the pure multiple and the conceptual propositions that today can found philosophy again. I did this under the general hypothesis that the thinking of being *qua* being is accomplished in mathematics and that, to embrace its conditions and make them compossible, philosophy must determine the 'what-is-not-being-*qua*-being', which I designated as 'event'. The concept of genericity is introduced to give an account of the effects, internal to a multiple-situation, of an event supplementing it. It designates the status of certain multiplicities, which are simultaneously inscribed in a situation and consistently weave within it chance irreversibly subtracted from all forms of naming. This multiple-intersection of the regulated consistency of a situation and the eventful randomness supplementing it is quite precisely the locus of a truth of the situation. This truth results from an infinite procedure. What we can say of it is only, assuming the completion of the procedure, that it 'will have been' generic, or indiscernible.

My purpose here is only to indicate *why* it is reasonable to consider that a generic multiple is the type of being of a truth. Given a multiple, that is, something whose entire being is pure multiple, multiple-without-One, how can the being of what makes truth of such a multiple be thought? That is the crux of the matter. Inasmuch as the unfathomable depths of what is present is inconsistency, a truth will be that which, from inside the presented, as *part* of this presented, makes the inconsistency—which buttresses in the last instance the consistency of presentation—come into the light of day. What is maximally subtracted from consistency, from the rule that dominates and represses the pure multiple (a rule I call the 'count-as-one'), can only be an especially 'evasive', indistinct multiple, without contours, without any possible explicit naming. Exemplarily, so to speak, *any* multiple *whatsoever*. If one wishes to maintain in one flail swoop that the authority of the multiple as to being is unlimited and that there is truth, this truth must obey three criteria:

— As this truth must be the truth *of a multiple*, and this without recourse to the transcendence of the One, it must be a production that is *immanent* to this multiple. A truth shall be a part of the initial multiple, of the situation of which there is truth.

— As being is multiple, and truth must *be*, a truth shall be a multiple, thus a multiple-part of the situation of which it is the truth. As might be expected, it cannot be an 'already' given or present part. It shall stem from a singular procedure. In fact, this procedure can only be set into motion from the point of a supplement, something in excess of the situation, that is, an event. A truth is the infinite result of a risky supplementation. Every truth is post-eventful. In particular, there is no 'structural' or objective truth. Concerning structural statements admissible in the situation, we shall never say that they are true but only that they are veridical. They are related not to truth, but to knowledge.

— As the being of the situation is its inconsistency, a truth about this being shall be presented as any multiplicity whatsoever, an anonymous part or consistency reduced to presentation as such, without a namable predicate or singularity. A truth shall thus be a generic part of the situation, 'generic' designating that it is any part whatsoever of it, that it says nothing in particular about the situation, except precisely its multiple-being as such, its fundamental inconsistency. A truth is this minimal consistency (a part, a conceptless immanence), which certifies in the situation the inconsistency from which its being is made. But since at the outset every part of the situation is presented as singular, namable, regulated in accordance with consistency, the generic part that a truth is shall have to be produced. It shall constitute the infinite multiple-horizon of a post-eventful procedure, which shall be called a generic procedure.

Poem, matheme, inventive politics and love are quite precisely the different possible types of generic procedures. What they produce (the unnamable in language itself, the potency of the pure letter, general will as the anonymous force of every namable will and the Two of the sexes as what has never been counted as one) in variable situations is never but a truth of these situations under the species of a generic multiple, onto which no knowledge can 'pin' its name, or discern beforehand its status.

From such a concept of truth, as the post-eventful production of a generic multiple of the situation whose truth it is, we can take up the constitutive triad of modern philosophy again: Being, subject and truth. Concerning being *qua* being, we will hold that mathematics historically constitutes the only possible thinking, inasmuch as it is the infinite inscription of the pure multiple, of the predicateless multiple in the empty potency of the letter, and that this is essential to what is given and grasped in its presentation. Mathematics is actual ontology. Concerning truth, we will hold that it is suspended to the singular supplementation constituted by the event. Its being, multiple like the being of all that is, is the being of any generic indiscernible part whatsoever, which, executing the multiple in the anonymity of its multiplicity, pronounces its being. Concerning the subject, at last, we will hold that it is a *finite moment* of the generic procedure. In this way, it is noteworthy that we must conclude that a subject exists only in the strict order of one of the four types of genericity. Every subject is artistic, scientific, political or amorous. Something that, besides, everyone knows from experience, for out of these registers, there is only existence, or individuality, but no subject.

Genericity, at the conceptual heart of a Platonic gesture turned toward the multiple, founds the inscription and compossibility of the contemporary conditions of philosophy. What we know about inventive politics at least since 1793, when it exists, is that it can only be egalitarian and anti-Statist, tracing, in the historic and social thick, humanity's genericity, the deconstruction of strata, the ruin of differential or hierarchical representations and the assumption of a communism of singularities. What we know about poetry is that it explores an unseparated, non-instrumental language, offered to everyone, a voice founding the genericity of speech itself. What we know about the matheme is that it seizes the multiple stripped of every presentative distinction, the genericity of multiple-being. What we know about love, at last, is that beyond the encounter, it declares its fidelity to the pure Two it founds and makes generic truth of the fact that there are men and women.

Philosophy today is the thinking of the generic as such, which begins, which has begun, for "A magnificence shall be deployed, whichever comes, analogous to the Shadow of old".[1]

THE (RE)TURN OF
PHILOSOPHY ITSELF

THE (RE)TURN OF
PHILOSOPHY ITSELF[1]

Let us name the inaugural statement 'Thesis 1' in homage to our masters' (and especially Louis Althusser's) assertive style. It nonetheless has the form of a negative report:

1. *Philosophy today is paralyzed by its relation to its own history.*

This paralysis results from the fact that, philosophically examining the history of philosophy, our contemporaries almost all concur to declare that this history has entered the perhaps interminable epoch of its closure. The upshot of this is a 'malaise in philosophy', and what I shall name a relocalization: philosophy no longer knows whether it has a suitable place. It seeks to be grafted onto established activities: art, poetry, science, political action, psychoanalysis... Or else, philosophy is now nothing *but* its own history. It becomes its own museum. I call paralysis of philosophy this zigzagging between historiography and relocalization. It is certain that this paralysis is closely linked to the constant and pessimistic relation of philosophy to its glorious metaphysical past.

The dominant idea is that metaphysics has been historically depleted, but that the beyond of this depletion has not yet been given to us. It is in this sense that I understand Heidegger's assertion in his testimonial interview: "*Only a God can save us.*"[2] Heidegger is most certainly not waiting for a new religion. He means the salvation of thought cannot be in continuity with its prior philosophical effort. *Something* has to *happen*, and the word 'God' designates this unheard-of, incalculable event, alone able from now on to render thought to its original destination. Philosophy is then caught between the depletion of its historical possibility and the conceptless advent of a salvational turnabout. Contemporary philosophy combines the deconstruction of its past and the empty awaiting of its future.

My whole purpose is to break with this diagnosis. The difficulty of this purpose is to avoid the neoclassical style, the conventionalist style, of those who intend to fill the gap with meager reflections on ethics.

We must go back to the roots and the roots are the reflexive, almost parasitic node, linking philosophy and historiography. The thesis I am defending will thus take a second form, one of rupture. Let us call it Thesis 2. It shall be formulated in the following way:

2. *Philosophy must break, from within itself, with historicism.*

To break with historicism—what meaning does this injunction have? We mean philosophic presentation must initially determine itself without reference to its history. It must be bold enough to present its concepts without first bringing them in front of the tribunal of their historic moment.

At bottom, Hegel's famous formula still hangs over us: "The history of the world is also the tribunal of the world." Today, the history of philosophy is more than ever its tribunal, and this tribunal almost constantly returns a verdict of capital punishment: it is the verdict of the closure or the necessary deconstruction of the metaphysical past and present. It can be said that Nietzsche's genealogical method, just as Heidegger's hermeneutic method, have only proposed variants of the Hegelian apparatus on this point. For, as with Nietzsche so also with Heidegger, it is true that all thought declaring itself philosophical must first be *evaluated* within a historical montage.[1] As with Nietzsche so also with Heidegger, this historical montage has its motivating force with the Greeks. For both of them, the game is played, the starting bell rung in what takes place *between* the Presocratics and Plato. A first destination of thought was therein lost and dominated, and this loss dictates our destiny.

I propose to tear philosophy away from this genealogical imperative. Heidegger believes we are historically directed by the forgetting of being, and even by the forgetting of this forgetting. I shall propose for my part a violent *forgetting of the history of philosophy*, thus a violent forgetting of the whole historical montage of the oblivion of being. A 'forget the forgetting of the forgetting'. This imperative of forgetting is a method, and, of course, in no way is it an ignoring. To forget history—this at first means to make *decisions of thinking* without returning to a supposed historical sense prescribed by these decisions. It is a question of breaking with historicism to enter, as someone like Descartes or Spinoza did, into an autonomous legitimating of discourse. Philosophy must take on axioms of thinking and draw consequences from them. It is only then, and from its immanent determination, that it will summon its history.

Philosophy must determine itself in such a way as to judge its history *itself*, and not have its history judge it.

Today such an operation of forgetting history and of axiomatic invention supposes we accept to *define* philosophy. To define it, precisely, other than from its history, other than from the destiny and decline of Western metaphysics. I shall thus propose a third form of my thesis, this time resolutely affirmative:

3. A definition of philosophy exists.

Let me add that in my view this definition is itself an historic *invariant*. It is not a definition in terms of a result, or the production of a loss of sense. It is an intrinsic definition enabling one to distinguish philosophy from what is not philosophy, and this, since Plato. It can also be distinguished from what is not philosophy but *resembles* it, resembles it a great deal, and which, since Plato, we call sophistry.

This question of sophistry is very important. The sophist is from the outset the enemy-brother, philosophy's implacable twin. Philosophy today, caught in its historicist malaise, is very weak in the face of modern sophists. Most often, it even considers the great sophists—for there are great sophists—as great philosophers. Exactly as if we were to consider that the great philosophers of Antiquity were not Plato and Aristotle, but Gorgias and Protagoras. An argument which is moreover increasingly defended, and often brilliantly, by modern historiographers of Antiquity.

Who are the modern sophists? The modern sophists are those that, in the footsteps of the great Wittgenstein, maintain that thought is held to the following alternative: either effects of discourse, language games, or the silent indication, the pure 'showing' of something subtracted from the clutches of language. Those for whom the fundamental opposition is not between truth and error or wandering, but between speech and silence, between what can be said and what is impossible to say. Or between statements endowed with meaning and others devoid of it.

In many regards, what is presented as the most contemporary philosophy is a potent sophistry. It ratifies the final statement of the *Tractatus*—"Whereof one cannot speak, thereof one must be silent"[3]— whereas philosophy exists only to defend that the whereof one cannot speak is precisely what it sets out to say.

The objection will be raised that, in its essential movement, contemporary discourse itself also claims to break with historicism, at least in its Marxist or Humanist form; that it goes against the ideas of progress and the avant-garde; that it declares, along with Lyotard, that the epoch of the Grand Narratives is over. To be sure. But this discourse only draws from its 'postmodernist' rebuttal a kind of general equivalence of discourses, a rule of virtuosity and obliquity. It attempts to compromise the very idea of truth in the fall of historic narratives. Its critique of Hegel is actually a critique of philosophy itself, to the benefit of art, or Right, or an immemorial or unutterable Law. This is why it must be said that this discourse, which adjusts the multiplicity of the registers of meaning to some silent correlate, is nothing but modern sophistry. That such a completely productive and virtuosic discourse should be taken for a philosophy demonstrates the philosopher's inability today to practice a firm, founding delimitation between him- or herself and the sophist.

The modern sophist attempts to replace the idea of truth with the idea of rule. Such is the most profound sense of Wittgenstein's otherwise inspired undertaking. Wittgenstein is our Gorgias, and we respect him as such. The ancient sophist had already replaced truth with the mixture of force and convention. The modern one wants to set the strength of the rule, and, more broadly, modalities of the linguistic authority of the Law against the revelation or production of the true.

A recent avatar of this will is the requisitioning of the Jewish epic, which has become in a few years the paradigm whose potency is extended well beyond the political sphere, and which today has to be considered as a veritable philosopheme.

It is not certain that the grandeur and tragedy of this epic is exactly appropriate to the ends pursued by the discourse of the modern sophist. But, *volens nolens*, 'the Jews' lend to contemporary discourse what without 'them' would be lacking—as with any fragmentary sophistry: historic depth. Postmodernity, having left behind the arrogance of progressive discourse, which it judges party to the redemption theme—and not without good reason—will readily oppose Jewish wandering, under the original authority of the law, to Christianism, which claims truth has actually *come*. The Jewish framework, about which we shall say–assuming its traditional setting-up, which is perilous—that it combines law and interpretation, thus contrasts with the Christian framework, combining faith and revelation.

I shall certainly not say that this way of thinking the split between Judaism and Christianism is well founded. In the first place, because the universal meaning of the signifier 'Jew' does not lend itself to representation by the religious narrative, even when brought to its greatest abstraction. Also, because Paul the Jew's thinking, located at the exact point at which the nexus of faith and law has to be decided, is otherwise complex. What interests me in this example is the *strategy* of modern sophistry: to stand language analysis against a historic and preferentially paradoxical Subject so that the sophistic denial of philosophy can *nonetheless* benefit from the modern prestige of historicism. It has to be recognized that this operation endows contemporary discourse with the cumulated energies of the hyper-critique of forms and the majesty of destiny.

From this postmodern suppleness of sophistry's, an obligation results for philosophy. For, restoring philosophy to itself by way of the oblivion of its history, suddenly necessarily implies that we give ourselves the wherewithal again to clearly distinguish the philosopher from the sophist. I shall say this in the form of a fourth thesis:

4. *Every definition of philosophy must distinguish it from sophistry.*

All in all, this thesis compels us to address the definition of philosophy by way of the concept of truth. For what the ancient or modern sophist claims to impose is precisely that there is no truth, that the concept of truth is useless and uncertain, since there are only conventions, rules, types of discourse or language games. We shall hence set down the variant of the fourth thesis, which I call 4b:

4b. *The category of truth is the central category, be it under another name, of any possible philosophy.*

Thus the necessity imposed by Thesis 2 to define philosophy becomes, in the light of the conflict with the modern sophist, the necessity to elucidate the intra-philosophic status of the category of truth.

Such an elucidation is presented—under the effect of axioms of thinking *activated* by its deployment—as the renewal of an imperative as to the *philosophein*, which goes back to Parmenides and Plato. From this point of view, it works against the current of the century's becoming, this becoming whose data philosophy has claimed to harbor.

What should be retained of this century in its decline? What should be retained if we consider it from a *bird's-eye view*? Doubtless, three dispositions of History, three loci and three ideological complexes of philosophical dimensions—or pretensions.

The three dispositions are Stalinian bureaucratic socialism, the adventure of the fascisms and the 'Western' deployment of parliamentarisms.

The three loci are Russia, Germany and the United States.

The three complexes are dialectical materialism, that is, the philosophy of Stalinian Marxism, Heidegger's thinking in its militant National Socialist dimension and the American academic philosophy developed from the logical positivism of the Vienna Circle.

Stalinian Marxism declared the fusion of dialectical materialism and the real movement of History. Heidegger believed he discerned in Hitler's accession the moment when thought finally faces the planetary reign of technology, or the moment, as he stated in his Rectoral Address, when "we submit to the distant command of the beginning of our spiritual-historical existence."[4] Finally, Anglo-Saxon analytical philosophy finds in the examination of language and its rules a form of thinking compatible with democratic conversation.

A striking common feature of these three intellectual attempts is to assume a violent opposition to the Platonic foundation of metaphysics.

For Stalinian Marxism, Plato names the birth of idealism, a quasi-invariant figure of the philosophy of the oppressors.

For Heidegger, Plato names the moment of the launching of metaphysics. Being, with the Presocratics, "is" in the sense that it deploys itself as *phusis*. With Plato, it submits to and is obliterated in the *Form* or the *Idea*. It attains the steadfastness of Presence, whereby the substitution is prepared of the cross-cut problematic of the supreme existent to the authentic question and care of Being. What at the height of distress can dis-close the (re)beginning of thought must also turn us away from the Platonic launching.

The analytic and moderate operation of Anglo-Saxon philosophy seems at opposite ends to Heidegger's etymological and historical meditation. However, it too assigns to Plato a realist and obsolete vision of mathematical objects, an underestimation of the impact of the forms of language on thought, a metaphysics of the supra-sensible. In a certain sense, Heidegger and Carnap both undertook to ruin metaphysics or bring it to a close. Their procedures of critical thinking, whose methods are so divergent, nonetheless both designate Plato as the emblem of what must be overcome in philosophy.

All in all, Nietzsche was right when he announced that Europe would be cured of what he called "the Plato disease". For such is indeed the real content of contemporary statements about the end of philosophy, or the end of metaphysics. The content is the following: What was historically initiated by Plato has entered into the final moments of its effect.

As for myself, I believe the end of this End must be announced, or stated.

Stating the end of the End, of *this* End, inevitably amounts to reopening the Plato question. Not in order to restore the prescriptive figure from which modernity wants to be subtracted, but to examine whether it is not by an *other* Platonic *gesture* that our future thinking must be supported.

With Plato, what has struck me for a long time is the terrible turnabout that occurs between *Socrates' Apology* and, let us say, Book X of the *Laws*. For the Platonic meditation had been rooted in the question: Why was Socrates killed? Yet, it is completed in a sort of nocturnal terrorism, in a repressive apparatus that strikes out against impiety and the corrupters of youth—the very two counts of indictment that brought about Socrates' execution. As if it had to be said in the end that Socrates was legitimately put to death. It is truly significant that the one who says this in his *Laws* is called the Athenian. After Socrates, fictioned as his thinking life, comes the generic representative of the Polis, who once again pronounces against Socrates and in favor of the implacable fixity of criminal laws.[ii]

This turnabout makes me think there is not *one* Platonic foundation of philosophy, *one* inaugural gesture, for example the metaphysical gesture. But more so there is a setting-up of the philosophic apparatus, accompanied and escorted by a progressively excessive tension, *exposing* this apparatus to a sort of disaster.

So, I would like to meditate on this question: What originally exposes philosophy at its most extreme point to the disastrous induction that reverses its first data? A question also formulated as: What does Plato *give up on* in the trajectory leading from the aporetic dialogues to criminal prescriptions?

To answer this question, one must leave from the element in which philosophy institutes itself as a singular locus of thinking. The central category of 'classical' philosophy is definitely truth. But what is the status of this category? An attentive examination of Plato, which I cannot here retrace[5], led to the following theses:

1) *Prior* to philosophy, a 'prior to' that is not temporal, there are *truths*. These truths are heterogeneous, and proceed within the real independently of philosophy. Plato calls them "right opinions", or statements "from hypotheses" in the particular case of mathematics. These truths are related to four possible registers, systematically explored by Plato. The four plural loci, where a few truths 'insist', are mathematics, art, the political and the amorous encounter. Such are the factual, historic, or pre-reflexive conditions of philosophy.

2) Philosophy is a construction of thinking wherein the fact that there are truths is proclaimed *against sophistry*. But this central proclamation supposes a strictly philosophical category, *the* Truth. Through this category, both the 'there are' of truths and the *compossibility* of their plurality are declared, to which philosophy gives welcome and shelter. The Truth simultaneously designates a plural state of things (there are heterogeneous truths) *and* the unity of thought.

The statement 'there are truths' determines philosophy to the thinking of being.

The statement 'truths are, for thought, compossible' determines philosophy to the thinking of a unique time of thought, namely, what Plato calls "the always of time", or eternity, a strictly philosophical concept, which inevitably accompanies the setting-up of the category of Truth.[6]

Let us say: the contemporary renunciation of the notion of philosophical eternity, the cult of time, of Being-for-death and of finitude are obvious effects of historicism. Eternity in itself is in no way a religious

notion, but rather an essential notion of philosophy—
including and especially of atheistic philosophy, since
this notion alone affords placing philosophy under
the condition of the matheme. Renouncing eternity
amounts to preparing the triumph of the sophist, for
whom nothing has value but the finite act of stating,
such that it involves one in the normless disparity of
discourses.

3) The philosophical category of Truth is by itself
void. It operates but presents nothing. Philosophy is
not a production of truth, but an operation *from*
truths, an operation which disposes the 'there is' and
epochal compossibility of truths.

I established, in *L'Etre et l'Evénement*, the essential bond that exists between the void and being *qua*
being.[7] That the philosophical category of Truth is as
such void explains the primal crossing of philosophy
and ontology, that is, the ambiguous dialectic between
philosophy and mathematics. It is very important to
note that the void of the category of Truth (with a capital T), *is not the void of being*. For, it is an operational
void, and not a presented one. The only void presented
to thought is that of the mathematicians' empty set.
The void of Truth is, as we shall see, a simple *interval*
wherein philosophy operates on the truths external to
it. This void is thus not ontological. It is purely logical.

4) What is the structure of this operation ?

Philosophy proceeds universally to construct its
organic category—Truth—in two different and intricate ways.

— It relies on paradigms of sequential linking,
argumentative style, definitions, refutations, proofs
and conclusive strength. Let us say that, in this case,
it constructs the void of the category of Truth as the
reverse-side or inversion of a regulated succession.
With Plato, it is the regime of the 'long detour', dialec-

tical developments whose procedures are exactly the same as those of the sophists he combated. This rhetoric of succession does not constitute a field of knowledge, since we know full well that none of these 'proofs' has ever established a theorem of philosophy recognized by all. But it *resembles* knowledge, although its destination is actually constructive. In fact, it is not a matter of something being established or 'known', but rather of a category reaching the clarity of its construction. Knowledge is being imitated here for productive purposes. This is why we shall call this procedure, which is also the one of Descartes' Order of Concepts, or of the Spinozist *more geometrico*, a *fiction of knowledge*. Truth is the un-known of this fiction.

— Or else philosophy proceeds by metaphors, strength of the image and persuasive rhetoric. This time it is a matter of indicating the void of the category of Truth *as a limit-point*. Truth interrupts the succession, and is recapitulated over and above itself. With Plato, it is the images, myths and comparisons whose workings are the same as those of the poets he combated. Art is this time mobilized, not because it has worth in and of itself, or with an imitative and cathartic aim, but to raise the void of Truth up to the point at which dialectical sequential linking is suspended. Here again, it is in no way a question of 'making a work of art', but the text does resemble the latter and could even be handed down and felt as such, although its destination is completely different. It can be said that art is imitated in its ways, with the idea of producing a subjective site of Truth. Let us call the treatment at this limit a *fiction of art*. Truth is the unutterable of this fiction.

Philosophy borrows from its two long-standing opponents: the sophists and poets. Moreover, it can

also be said that it borrows from two truth procedures: mathematics, the paradigm of proof, and art,
the paradigm of subjective potency.[8] Its peculiar property is to borrow only in order to construct a categorical operation, which firmly fixes its locus.

The philosophic operation of the category of Truth
lays out sorts of pincers or tongs. One of the limbs of
these pincers is presented as an adjustment of the
successive by the argument. The other, as a declaration at the limit. Truth links and sublimates.

5) The pincers of Truth, which link and subli-
mate, have a duty to seize *truths*. The relation of
(philosophic) Truth to (scientific, political, artistic or
amorous) truths is one of *seizing*. By 'seizing', we
mean capture, hold, and also seizure, astonishment.
Philosophy is the locus of thinking wherein (non-
philosophic) truths are seized as such, and seize us.

The effect of seizing taken in its first sense aims
to deliver the compossibility of the plural of truths in
a persuasive way. They let themselves be seized
together by the pincers philosophy has put together
under the name of Truth (or any other equivalent
name, it is the function of seizing which matters). It is
not a question here, between Truth and truths, of a
relation of super-sumption, subsuming, founding or
guaranteeing. It is a relation of seizing: philosophy is
a pinch of truths.

The effect of seizing taken in its second sense dri-
ves philosophy with a singular intensity. This intensity
comes from love, but love without the quandaries of the
object of love, without the enigmas of its difference.

More generally, philosophy, because its central
category is void, is essentially *subtractive*.[9] Philosophy
must in fact subtract Truth from the maze of sense.
Within its heart, there is a lack, a hole. There is the
fact that the category of Truth and its time-bound

escort, eternity, refer to nothing in presentation. Philosophy is not an interpretation of the sense of what is offered to experience; philosophy is an operation of a category subtracted from presence. And this operation that seizes truths precisely indicates that, thus grasped, truths are distributed within what interrupts the regime of sense.

This point is, in my view, of capital importance. Philosophy is first and foremost a rupture with the narrative and with commentary about the narrative. By the dual effect of the pincers of Truth, by the argument that links and by the limit that sublimates, philosophy opposes the effect of Truth to the effect of sense. Philosophy separates itself from religion because it separates itself from hermeneutics.

All of this leads me to give the following provisional definition of philosophy:

Philosophy is the stirring up, under the category of Truth, of a void located in accordance with the inversion of a succession and the other-side of a limit. With this end in view, philosophy organizes the superimposition of a fiction of knowledge and a fiction of art. It constructs a device to seize truths, which means: to state that there are some, and to let itself be seized by this 'there are'; to thus aver the unity of thought. This seizing is driven by the intensity of love without an object, and composes a persuasive strategy without any stakes in power. This entire procedure is prescribed by conditions, those of art, science, love and the political, in their event figure. Finally, this procedure is polarized by a specific adversary, the sophist.

It is within the element of this definition that the rupture with historicism must be accomplished and the strict delimitation between the philosopher and the modern sophist be engaged.

The first task is obviously to take on the appraisal of the current becoming of truths, within the fourfold register of science, and particularly of modern mathematics; of the political, and particularly of the end of the epoch of revolutions; of love, and particularly of what introduces light, or shadows into it, psychoanalysis; of art, and particularly poetry since Rimbaud and Mallarmé. This course is all the more necessary since contemporary discourse being the standardbearer of the 'end of metaphysics' often prides itself—and this is also a typically sophistic trait—on being the one that is fully steeped in its time, being homogeneous to youth, to the liquidation of archaisms. In its pincers, it is indispensable that philosophy deal with the most active, the most recent, indeed the most paradoxical thinking material. But this very locating supposes axioms of thinking subtracted from the judgment of History, axioms allowing the construction of a category of Truth, which is innovative and appropriate for our time.

We can from then on philosophically envisage the determination of today's dominant 'philosophical' discourse as modern sophistry, and in consequence the determination of a just relation of thinking to the statements constituting it.

But before we turn to this determination, the following insistent question must be taken up again: Why does philosophy, such as we have specified its concept, recurrently expose thought to disaster? What leads philosophy from the aporia of the void of Truth to the legitimation of criminal prescriptions?

The key to this turnabout is that philosophy is worked from within by the chronic temptation of taking the operation of the empty category of Truth as identical to the multiple procedures of the production of truths. Or else: that philosophy, renouncing the operational singularity of the seizing of truths, is *itself* presented as being a truth procedure. Which also means that it is presented as an art, a science, a passion or a policy. Nietzsche's philosopher-poet; Husserl's wish of philosophy as a rigorous science; Pascal or Kierkegaard's wish of philosophy as intense existence; Plato's philosopher-king: as many intra-philosophical schemata of the permanent possibility of disaster. These schemata are all at the behest of the filling-in of the void that supports the practice of the pincers of Truth.

The disaster in philosophical thought is topical when philosophy is presented as being not a seizing of truths, but a *situation of truth.*

The effects of this filling-in of the void, or of its befalling to presence amounts to yielding on three points.

First of all, by being presented as the plenitude of Truth, philosophy gives up on the multiple of truths, the heterogeneity of their procedures. It avers that there is one single locus of Truth and that this locus is established by philosophy itself. It transforms the empty gap of the pincers of Truth—which is 'what there is' between linking and sublimation—into a spacing of being wherein Truth *is.*

Once there is *one* locus of Truth, there is a binding metaphor of the access to this locus. Acceding to the locus reveals it in its dazzling unicity. Philosophy is an initiation, a path, an access to what is open to the locus of Truth. There is ultimately an *ecstasy* of place. This ecstasy is obviously perceptible in the Platonic presentation of the intelligible place, *topos noètos.* The poetically imperative style of the Myth of Er the Pamphylian, at the end of the *Republic,* seeks to transmit the ecstatic access to the locus of Truth.

Secondly, philosophy that abandons itself to the substantialization of the category of Truth gives up on

the multiplicity of the *names* of Truth, on the temporal and variable dimension of these names. Theorems,
principles, declarations, imperative, beauty and laws:
such are a few of these names. But if *the* Truth is,
then there is but a single genuine name, an eternal
one. To be sure, eternity is always an attribute of the
category of Truth. But this attribute is only legitimate
insofar as the category is void, since it is only an
operation. If this category attests to a presence, then
eternity is projected onto the disparate of the names.
It institutes a unique Name, and this Name is inevitably *sacred*. The sacralization of the name ends up
doubling the ecstasy of place.

This sacralization certainly overdetermines the
idea of the Good with Plato. The idea of the Good has
two legitimate philosophical functions:

— it designates, over and above *ousia*, Truth as
limit. It thus names the second limb of the pincers of
Truth (the first is the dianoetic);

— it designates the essential point, which is that
there is no Truth of the Truth. There is a stopping
point, an irreflexive point, an empty otherness.

But the Idea of the Good has a third illegitimate,
excessive, doubtful function: when it operates as the
unique and sacred name to which *every* truth would
be suspended. Here the rigor of the philosophic operation is transgressed, overstepped and subverted.

Third and lastly, when it imagines itself producing truth, philosophy gives up on its moderation, its
critical virtue. It becomes a harrowing prescription,
an obscure and tyrannical commandment. Why?
Because philosophy then declares that the category of
Truth has befallen to presence. And as this presence
is that of *the* Truth what is outside of presence falls
within an imperative of annihilation.

Let us make this more explicit. Philosophy, driven over and above its operation, says: 'The void of Truth is presence'. So be it. But this void is *really* empty, for philosophy is not a truth procedure, it is not a science, nor an art, nor politics, nor love. So, this real void turns up in being, but as what, in the eyes of philosophy, is outside Truth, if Truth is presence. Something of being is presented as outside Truth, and hence something of being is presented *as having not to be*. When philosophy is the philosophy of the presence of Truth, presence placed over and above truths, then it says, necessarily: this, which is, must not be. A law of death accompanies the supposed coming-into-presence of the void of Truth.

Asserting that this, which is, must not be, or that what is presented is in its being but nothingness, is an effect of *terror*. The essence of terror is to pronounce the must-not-be of what is. Philosophy, when it is driven out of its operation by the temptation wielded upon it by the idea that Truth is substance produces terror, just as it produces ecstasy of the place and the sacred of the name.

It is exactly this triple knotted effect, of ecstasy, the sacred and terror, which I name *disaster*. It is a matter of *thought's* own disaster. But every empirical disaster originates in a disaster of thought. Every disaster has at its root a substantialization of Truth, that is, the 'illegal' passage of Truth as an empty operation to truth as the befalling-to-presence of the void itself.

Thus, philosophy opens the way to disaster. Reciprocally, every real and, in particular, every historic disaster contains a philosopheme that knots together ecstasy, the sacred and terror.

There are potent and identified forms of such philosophemes. Stalinian Marxism's new Proletarian

Man, National Socialism's historically destined German people are philosophemes, taken to unheard-of effects of terror against what does not have the right to be (the traitor to the cause, the Jew, the Communist...), and pronouncing the ecstasy of the place (the German Land, Socialism's Homeland) and the sacred of the Name (the Führer, the Father of peoples).

But there are flaccid and insidious forms. The civilized man of imperial parliamentary democracies is also a disastrous philosopheme. A place is ecstatically pronounced in this form (the West) and a name sacralized as unique (the Marketplace, Democracy). Terror is wielded against what is and should not be: the impoverished planet, the distant rebel, the non-Western and the immigrant nomad driven by radical abandonment towards affluent metropolises.

These are the empirical, historic destinations of disastrous philosophemes handed over to execution.

But whence does the disastrous overstepping of the categorical operation proceed within philosophy itself? What internal tension carries philosophy, the locus of thinking wherein the seizing of truths operates, off course toward a schema of the presence of Truth which exposes to disaster?

The key to the problem is in the nature and measure of the conflictive relation between philosophy and sophistry.

From its origins to the present day, the stakes in this conflict concern the function of truth in the heterogeneity of discourses or the style of the determination of thought by the rules of language. It is not, nor can it be, a war of annihilation, without thought being menaced by the greatest of perils. Nothing is more philosophically useful for us than contemporary sophistry. Philosophy must never abandon itself to anti-sophistic extremism. It goes astray when it nourishes the dark desire of finishing off the sophist *once and for all.* It is precisely the following point that, in my view, defines dogmatism: to claim that the sophist, since he is like a perverted double of the philosopher, *ought not to exist.* No, the sophist must only be assigned *to his place.*

If it is true that the sophist is the singular adversary of philosophy—and all the more so since his rhetoric is the *same*—it is also true that philosophy must forever endure the sophist's company and sarcasm.

For what does the sophist say?

— The sophist says there are no truths, that there are only technics for statements and loci of enunciation. It is philosophically legitimate to reply, by means of the operation of the empty category of Truth, that there are truths. It is no longer legitimate to say, as does the dogmatist, that there is a sole locus of Truth and that this locus is revealed by philosophy itself. Such a retort is excessive, overstrung and disastrous. It confuses the operational void of Truth with the donation of being. It transforms philosophy from the rational operation it must be into the dubious path of an initiation. It stops up the void of the operation of seizing with the ecstasy of a unique place wherein Truth befalls to the veiling of its offering. This is an imposture. Philosophy may raise the objection to the sophist of the local existence of truths; it goes astray when it proposes the ecstasy of a place of Truth.

— The sophist says there is a multiplicity of language games, that there is plurality and heterogeneity of names. It is philosophically legitimate to reply by constructing, by means of the category of Truth, a locus wherein thought indicates its unity of time. To show, by means of their seizing, that truths are compossible. It is no longer legitimate to say there is just one name for truths. It is dogmatic and ruinous to mix up the heterogeneous plurality of truths under the Name, though inevitably sacred, that philosophy gives to Truth.

— The sophist says that being *qua* being is inaccessible to the concept and to thought. It is philosophically legitimate to designate, and to think, the empty locus of the seizing of truths by means of the pincers of Truth. It is no longer legitimate to claim that, under the category of Truth, the void of being befalls to the unique thought of its act, or its destiny. To the sophists, philosophy must oppose the real of the truths whose seizing it carries out. It goes astray when it proposes the terroristic imperative of being-True as such.

The ethics of philosophy is basically to maintain the sophist as its adversary, to preserve *polemos*, dialectical strife. The disastrous moment is the one when philosophy declares the sophist *must* not be, the moment when it decrees the annihilation of its Other.

In the truly philosophical dialogues, Plato *rebuts* the sophists. He does it with respect for Protagoras, in a kind of violent comedy for Callicles or Thrasymacus. But the dialectic always includes what the sophist is saying.

In Book X of the *Laws*, Plato resorts to *debarring* the sophist by the somber knotted scheming of ecstasy, the sacred and terror. Plato then gives up on the ethics of philosophy and exposes the whole of his thinking to disaster.

The sophist is required at all times for philosophy to maintain its ethics. For the sophist is the one who reminds us that the category of Truth is void. Indeed, he only does it to negate truths, whereby he must be combated. But combated within the ethical norms of this combat. Philosophical extremism, a figure of disaster within thinking, strives for the annihilation of the sophist. But it is in fact to his triumph that it contributes and abets. For, if philosophy renounces its operation and its void, the category of Truth has only dogmatic terror left to establish itself. Against which, the sophists will have an easy time showing the compromises of philosophical desire with tyrannies.

This is the real problem facing us today. The idea of the End of philosophy is also the idea of the end of the category of Truth. This undoubtedly involves appraising the disasters of the century. Dogmatic terror has taken the shape of the State. The dogmatic philosopheme has ventured as far as to be embodied in the police and concentration camps. Loci have been exalted, sacred names psalmed. Disaster has compromised philosophy. The provisional ruin of any confidence in Marxism, just like the *affaire Heidegger*, are but avatars of this compromise.[iii] It can be seen what it has cost philosophy to renounce its void and eternity. Its operation. What it has cost philosophy to want to be *realized* within time.

However, asserting the end of philosophy and the irrelevance of Truth is strictly a *sophistic* appraisal of the century. We are attending a second anti-Platonic requital, for contemporary 'philosophy' is a generalized sophistry, which is moreover neither without talent nor without greatness. Language games, deconstruction, feeble thinking, irremediable heterogeneity, differends and differences, the ruin of Reason, the promotion of the fragment and discourse in shreds: all of these argue in favor of a sophistic line of thinking and place philosophy at an impasse.

Let us simply say: following the sophistic or postmodern appraisal of the disasters of the century comes a time of counter-sophistic appraising. And inasmuch as these disasters were born of the paroxysmal will of philosophy to be inscribed in History; inasmuch as the catastrophes of Truth come from the fact that, obsessed by its own past and its becoming, philosophy gave up on the void and on eternity: so it is legitimate that the new philosophical appraisal should be directed *against* the authority of history, against historicism.

The central point is to deploy the category of Truth again in its operation, in its ability to seize. This redeployment will integrate and surmount the objection of Great Modern Sophistry. Indeed, Truth must reconstruct its pincers by making room for the laws of language, chance, the indiscernible, the event and singularity. Philosophy must explicitly consider its central category as void. But philosophy must also maintain that this void is the condition of an actual operation. Philosophy must give up neither on sequential linking, as instructed by contemporary mathematics, nor on sublimation and limits, as instructed by modern poetry. The intensity of love will be enlightened by the logical twists and turns of psychoanalysis. Persuasive strategy will be enlightened by the debate on politics and democracy.

This shall be the fifth variation on my thesis. It is said quite simply as:

5. Philosophy is possible.

Whence follows the variant of this variant—let us state it as 5b:

5b. Philosophy is necessary.

This is not a question here of the history of philosophy. Not one of ideology. Nor even one of æsthetics, an epistemology or a political sociology. Not a question of the examination of the rules of language. It is a question of philosophy *itself,* in its singular delimitation, in its conformity to the definition I have proposed. It is a question of philosophy such as it was instituted by Plato.

We can and we must write a *Republic* and a *Symposium* for our contemporaries. Just as, for the major sophists, there were a *Gorgias* and a *Protagoras*, so must there be a *Nietzsche* and a *Wittgenstein*. And, for the minor sophists, a *Vattimo* and a *Rorty*. No more nor any less polemical, no more nor any less respectful.

Philosophy is possible, philosophy is necessary. And yet for it to be, it must be desired. Philippe Lacoue-Labarthe says that History—he is thinking of Nazi barbarism—henceforth forbids us the desire of philosophy.[10] I cannot grant him this, for such a conviction puts the philosopher at the very outset in a position of weakness with respect to modern sophistry. Another way out is possible: to desire philosophy against history, to break with historicism. Philosophy then re-appears as what it is, a bright opening of eternity, without God or soul, from the very fact that its effort puts us in agreement with the following: that there are truths. Such is the orientation of what I do not hesitate to consider, for thought, as a *duty*. And if I compare, as does Mallarmé, the eternal void of philosophical Truth to a bed of ideal and thus inexistent flowers, to irises whose genus— "the family of irises"—exists only in the philosopher's operation, I shall say along with him, mixing exaltation and dictate—just as Truth superimposes a fiction of art onto a fiction of knowledge:

Glory of long desire, Ideas
Everything in me was exalted to see
The family of irises
Burgeoning to this new responsibility.[11]

Such a burgeoning, such a re-turn of affirmative thinking are wagers also. Mallarmé, again: "Every thought emits a throw of the dice". Let us throw the dice of philosophy. When the dice fall, there will still be time to discuss, with modern sophists, what Mallarmé calls "the total count in the making".[12]

DEFINITION OF PHILOSOPHY

DEFINITION OF PHILOSOPHY[1]

Philosophy is prescribed by conditions that are the types of truth procedures or generic procedures. These types are science (more precisely the matheme), art (more precisely the poem), the political (more precisely the political in its interiority, or politics of emancipation) and love (more precisely the procedure which makes truth out of the disjunction of sexuated positions).

Philosophy is the locus of thinking wherein the 'there are' truths is stated, along with their compossibility. To this end, it constructs an operational category, Truth, which opens an active void within thought. This void is located according to the inversion of a succession (the style of argumentative expounding) and the other-side of a limit (the style of persuasive or subjectivating expounding). Philosophy, as discourse, thus assembles the superimposition of a fiction of knowledge and a fiction of art.

In the void opened by the gap or interval of the two fictionings[1], philosophy *seizes* truths. This seizing is its act. By this act, philosophy declares that there are truths, and works in such a way as to have thought seized by this 'there are'. This seizure by the act testifies to the unity of thought.

As a fiction of knowledge, philosophy imitates the matheme. As a fiction of art, it imitates the poem. As the intensity of an act, it is like a love without an object. Addressed to everyone so that they all participate in the seizure of the existence of truths, it is like a political strategy without any stakes in power.

Through this fourfold discursive imitation, philosophy knots together within itself the system of its conditions. This is the reason for which *a* philosophy is homogeneous to the stylistics of its epoch. However, this permanent contemporaneity is orientated not toward empirical time, but toward what Plato calls "the always of time", the timeless essence of time, which philosophy names eternity.[2] The philosophical seizing of truths exposes them to eternity—we can say along with Nietzsche, the eternity of their *return*. This eternal exposure is all the more real since truths are seized with the utmost urgency and extreme precariousness of their temporal path.

The act of seizing, such as an eternity orientates it, roots out truths from the gangue of sense. It *separates* them from the law of the world. Philosophy is subtractive in that it makes a hole in sense, or makes an interruption in the circulation of sense, for truths to all be *said* together. Philosophy is an insensate act, and by this very fact rational.

Philosophy is never an interpretation of experience. It is the act of Truth with respect to truths. And this act, which is unproductive according to the law of the world (it does not even produce one truth), disposes a subject without an object, a subject open only to truths transiting in its seizure.

Let us call 'religion' everything that presupposes continuity between truths and the circulation of sense. It will then be said: against any hermeneutic, that is, against the religious law of sense, philosophy disposes compossible truths with the void as background. Thus, it subtracts thought from every presupposition of Presence.

The subtractive operations whereby philosophy seizes truths 'out of sense' is related to four modalities: the undecidable, related to the event (a truth is not, it befalls); the indiscernible, related to liberty (the path of a truth is not constrained, but risky); the generic, related to being (the being of a truth is an infinite set subtracted from every predicate in knowledge); the unnamable, related to the Good (to force the naming of an unnamable breeds disaster).

The schema of connection of the four figures of the subtractive (the undecidable, the indiscernible, the generic and the unnamable) specifies a philosophical doctrine of Truth. This schema disposes the thinking of the void as the background on which truths are seized.

The whole philosophical procedure is polarized by a specific adversary, the sophist. The sophist is externally (or discursively) indiscernible from the philosopher since his operation also combines fictions of knowledge and fictions of art. Subjectively, he is opposed to the philosopher since his linguistic strategy aims at avoiding any positive assertion concerning truths. In this way, philosophy can also be defined as the act whereby indiscernible discourses are nonetheless opposed. Or else as what separates itself from its double. Philosophy is always the breaking of a mirror. This mirror is the surface of language, on which the sophist sets everything that philosophy treats in its act. If the philosopher claims to contemplate himself on this sole surface, he sees his double, the sophist, suddenly spring forth from it and can thus take himself for the sophist.

This relation to the sophist inwardly exposes philosophy to a temptation whose effect is to split it in two again. For the desire of finishing off the sophist *once and for all* thwarts the seizing of truths: 'once and for all' inevitably means that Truth annuls the randomness of truths, and that philosophy unduly declares itself a producer of truths. Whereby *being-true* comes into the position of doubling the *act* of Truth.

A threefold effect of the sacred, ecstasy and terror then corrupts the philosophical operation, and may lead it, from the aporetic void sustaining its act, to criminal prescriptions. Whence philosophy is inductive of every disaster in thought.

The ethics of philosophy, staving off disaster, can be summarized in its constant *reserve* regarding its sophistic double, a reserve thanks to which philosophy is subtracted from the temptation of splitting itself into two (according to the void/substance couple) in order to deal with the first duplicity founding it (sophist/philosopher).

The history of philosophy is the history of its ethics: a succession of violent gestures through which philosophy is withdrawn from its disastrous redoubling. More precisely: philosophy in its history is but a desubstancialization of Truth, which is also the self-liberation of its act.

CHAPTER NOTES

Introduction

1. Paul Cohen, *Set Theory and the Continuum Hypothesis*, W. A. Benjamin, 1966.

2. See footnote five of "The (Re)turn of Philosophy Itself", page 123 of the present collection.

3. Alain Badiou, *L'Etre et l'événement*, Paris: Seuil, 1988, p. 14. (This work has yet to be translated.)

4. D. Janicaud, "France: Rendre à nouveau raison?" in *La Philosophie en Europe*, under the direction of R. Klibansky and David Pears, Paris: Gallimard/Folio, 1993, p. 187ff.

5. A. Badiou, "L'écriture du générique: Samuel Beckett" in *Conditions*, Paris: Seuil, 1992, p. 332.

6. A. Badiou, *L'Etre et l'événement*, op. cit., p. 20.

7. Ibid., p. 17. The term 'debar' is the translation of *forclusion*, the Freudian *Verwerfung* category as taken up by Lacan.

8. See below A. Badiou, *Manifesto for Philosophy*, chap. 3.

9. A. Badiou, "L'Entretien de Bruxelles" in *Les Temps Modernes*, May 1990, n° 526, p. 2.

10. A. Badiou, *L'Etre et l'événement, op. cit.*, p. 224.

11. A. Badiou, "L'écriture du générique: Samuel Beckett" in *Conditions, op. cit.*, p. 333.

12. A. Badiou, *L'Etre et l'événement, op. cit.*, p. 42. In the essay on Samuel Beckett, Badiou specifies the opposition between naming and hermeneutic interpretation: "Beckett replaces the initial hermeneutics [in his writings prior to 1960], which attempted to pin the event onto the network of meanings, by a completely different operation, naming. In light of a hazardous supplementing of being, naming seeks no sense. It sets out to draw an invented name from the very void of that which befalls. Interpretation is followed by poetic naming, which has no objective other than to *fasten* the incident and preserve a trace of its separation in language." "L'écriture du générique: Samuel Beckett" in *Conditions, op. cit.*, p. 350.

13. Stéphane Mallarmé, "Quant au livre: L'Action restreinte", in *Poésies. Anecdotes ou Poèmes, Pages diverses.* Paris: Le Livre de Poche, 1977, p. 210.

14. A. Badiou, *L'Etre et l'événement, op. cit.*, p. 418. The explanation given here of "the theory of canonical names for elements of the fundamental situation S as well as an indiscernible part" is a very brief summing up of the demonstration given by Badiou in "Meditation 34".

15. Ibid., p. 421.

16. Ibid., p. 423.

17. See below *Manifesto for Philosophy*, p. 36.

18. A. Badiou, "L'Entretien de Bruxelles" in *Les Temps Modernes*, Mai 1990, n° 526, p. 26.

19. Ibid., p. 26. (My emphasis).

20. Alan Badiou interviewed by Roger Pol-Droit: "Nous pouvons redéployer la philosophie" in *Le Monde*, 31 August 1993. Re-edited in *Les Grands entretiens du Monde*, Mai 1994, p. 29.

21. Arthur Kroker has theorized the notion of panic within the context of French poststructuralist thought. See especially, "Panic Doublings/Panic Materialism" in *The Possessed Individual. Technology and the French Postmodern*, Montreal: New World Perspectives/Culture Text series, 1992, pp. 117–120.

22. Once again from his essay on Beckett, Badiou adds: "*Verily* (and not following opinion), love depends on the pure event, the encounter, whose force radically exceeds both sentimentality and sexuality. The encounter founds the Two as such. In the figure of love, such that the origin encounters it, the Two *overcomes*, which includes the Two of the sexes or sexed figures. Love is in no way what makes One of a prior Two 'that would be its romantic version, which Beckett never tires of gibing at'. Love is never a fusion nor an effusion. It is the condition, often a laborious one, of the fact that the Two may exist as Two." "L'écriture du générique: Samuel Beckett" in *Conditions*, *op. cit.*, p. 358.

23. A. Badiou, "L'Entretien de Bruxelles" in *Les Temps Modernes*, *op. cit.*, p. 5.

24. See Gottlob Frege, "Function and Concept" in *Translations from the Philosophical Writings of Gottlob Frege*, edited by P. Geach and M. Black. Essay translated by Geach, Oxford: Basil Blackwell, 1970, p. 30.

25. A. Badiou, *L'Etre et l'événement*, Annexes: "The Axiom of the Empty Set: There exists a set that has no elements. This set is unique and has the mark 'ø' as its name."

26. François Wahl, "La Soustraction" Preface to Alain Badiou, *Conditions*, *op. cit.*, 1992, p. 53.

27. See below, "Definition of philosophy", p. 119.

Manifesto for Philosophy

1. Possibility

1. "Il ne faut plus être en désir de philosophie". Philippe Lacoue-Labarthe, *La Fiction du politique. Heidegger, l'art et la politique.* Paris: Christian Bourgois, 1987, p. 19.

2. "La philosophie comme architecture est ruinée". Jean-François Lyotard, *Le Différend.* Paris: Minuit, 1983. (English translation by G. Van den Abbeele.)

2. Conditions

1. Alain Badiou, *L'Etre et l'événement, op. cit.* As mentioned in the opening remarks, this text has yet to be translated.

2. Martin Heidegger, *Introduction to Metaphysics.* Trans. Ralph Manheim. New Haven, Conn.: Yale University Press, 1959. See chapter 1: "The Fundamental Question of Metaphysics".

3. Modernity

1. "La subjectivité est poussée vers son accomplissement". Martin Heidegger, "Wozu Dichter?" in *Holzwege.* Frankfort am Main: Vittorio Klostermann, 1949.

2. Martin Heidegger from the interview he gave to the German weekly, *Der Spiegel,* in 1966 under agreement of a posthumous publication. In France, it was published as *Réponses et questions sur l'histoire et la politique.* Trans. Jean Launay. Paris: Mercure de France, 1977.

4. Heidegger Viewed as Commonplace

1. "Le fait même que l'homme devienne sujet et le monde objet n'est qu'une conséquence de l'essence de la

technique en train de s'installer." Martin Heidegger, "Wozu Dichter?" in *Holzwege*. Frankfort am Main: Vittorio Klostermann, 1949.

2. Martin Heidegger from the testimonial interview he gave to the German weekly *Der Spiegel* in 1966.

5. Nihilism?

1. "Sur ce taureau de fer qui fume et qui beugle, l'homme a monté trop tôt." A. Vigny, "La Maison du berger", in *Destinées*, Paris: Gallimard, the "nrf/poésies" series, 1972.

2. K. Marx, "The Communist Manifesto," trans. David McLellan, in *Karl Marx: Selected Writings*, London: Oxford University Press, 1977, p. 223. The translation has been modified.

6. Sutures

1. See Jean-François Lyotard, *The Differend*, op. cit., § 98.

2. *visage*. see Emmanuel Levinas, *Totalité et infini. Essai sur l'extériorité*. Paris: Martinus Nijhoff, 1971.

7. The Age of Poets

1. Michel Deguy, poet and philosopher, has published *Poèmes (1960–1970)*, Paris: Gallimard, the "nrf/poésies" series, 1972.

2. Arthur Rimbaud, "Letter to Paul Demeny, 15 May 1871," in *Works*. Trans. Oliver Bernard. London: Penguin Classics, 1970. "Des faibles se mettraient à *penser* sur la première lettre de l'alphabet, qui pourraient vite ruer dans la folie!".

3. Isadore Ducasse (Compte of Lautréamont), *Songs of Maldoror*, II: 10. Trans. Paul Knight. London: Penguin Classics, 1978. "O mathématiques sévères, je ne vous ai pas oubliées, depuis que vos savantes leçons, plus douces

que le miel, filtrènt dans mon cœur, comme une onde rafraîchissante. Sans vous, dans ma lutte contre l'homme, j'aurais peut-être été vaincu."

4. Alvero de Campos (Fernando Pessoa), *Selected Poems*. Trans. Jonathan Griffin. London: Penguin Classics, 1974 (2nd edition, 1982), p. 126. (This poem was originally left untitled by Pessoa writing under one of his heteronyms, Alvero de Campos. In the Penguin edition, however, it has been given the title "Newton's Binomial".)

5. The evocation of this power of poets and thinkers is found in the *Der Spiegel* testemonial interview published in French as *Réponses et questions sur l'histoire et la politique*. Trans. Jean Launay, *op. cit.*, 1977, p. 46.

6. Arthur Rimbaud, *A Season in Hell*. Trans. by Paul Schmitt, N.Y. Harper and Row, 1967.

8. Events

1. G. Cantor, *Gesammelte Abhandlungen mathematischen und philosophischen Inhalts*. Springer-Verlag, 1980. P.J. Cohen, *Set Theory and the Continuum Hypothesis*. W.A. Benjamin, 1966.

2. "L'être comme tel, c'est l'amour qui vient à y aborder dans la rencontre". J. Lacan, *Séminaire XX—"Encore" (1972–1973)*, The 26 June 1973 session: "Le Rat dans le labyrinthe". Paris: Seuil, 1975, p. 133 (the original French edition).

3. J. Lacan, *Séminaire XX—Encore*, among other places: The 20 February 1973 session, "Dieu et la jouissance de la femme", p. 68 and the 10 April 1973 session, "Savoir et vérité", p. 94 of the French edition. Readers of Lacan's work will be familiar with the variations of what is essentially a logico-mathematical formula, thought up by Lacan. It is one of the two formulae of sexuation symbolizing the feminine: $\neg \chi \Phi(\chi)$ (not-all x is a function of phi, the phallus). This formula gives rise to the ambiguity of any fixed translation of *pas tout* as 'not-whole', or as 'not-all'.

Let us say that not-whole suggests the provocative meaning, whereas not-all suggests the intended meaning. I have decided to follow suit with Jacqueline Rose's translation of 'not-all'. See *Feminine Sexuality. Jacques Lacan and the école freudienne*. Edited by Juliet Mitchell and Jacqueline Rose. Trans. Jacqueline Rose. New York: Pantheon Books, 1985.

4. Sylvain Lazarus, political theoretician, teaches at University of Paris 8 (Vincennes at Saint-Denis). He has published *L'Anthropologie du nom*, Paris: Seuil, 1996.

5. An English translation of Paul Celan's "Anabasis" can be found in *Poems of Paul Celan*. Trans. by Michael Hamburger. New York: Persea books, 1972, p. 172. The German text reads:

[...]—wahre
Hinauf und Zurück
in die herzhelle Zukunft.

[...]

werdende Zeltwort :
Mitsammen.

9. Questions

1. J. Lacan, "La science et la vérité," *Écrits II*, Paris: Senil, 1966, p. 228.

2. Ludwig Wittgenstein, *Tractatus Logico-philosophicus*. Trans. C.K. Ogden. London: Routledge and Kegan Paul, 1922.

10. Platonic Gesture

1. The following excerpts are taken from the preface of F. Nietzsche's *Beyond Good and Evil*, translation by Walter Kaufmann, Princeton: Princeton University Press, 1983.

11. Generic

1. "Une magnificence se déploiera, quelconque, analogue à l'Ombre de jadis." Stéphane Mallarmé, "Offices:

catholicisme" in *Igitur—Divagations—Un Coup de dés.* Paris: Gallimard, the "nrf/poésies" series, 1945, p. 291.

The (Re)turn of Philosophy *Itself*

1. "This text," writes Alain Badiou, "has composite origins, and its reorganization almost makes it an original one.

The first source is a paper given in Italy in the spring of 1990 for a colloqium organized by the philosophy department of the University of Pavia. My title then was *The end of the End.*

A first recasting resulted in the text of a conference held in Spain, at the invitation of the Catalan association, *Acta,* located in Barcelona. However, at the last moment, and given the nature of the audience, I chose against giving this paper, and substituted something entirely different.

Finally, during the first semester of my 1990–1991 seminar at the Collège international de philosophie (Paris), I took up even more developments."

2. See the M. Heidegger *Der Spiegel* interview, mentioned above in chapter 3, footnote 2.

3. Wittgenstein, *Tractatus-Logico Philosophicus,* op. cit.

4. M. Heidegger, "The Rectoral Address" in *Martin Heidegger and National Socialism—Questions and Answers,.* Trans: Lisa Nerris. Collection edited by Gunther Neske and Emil Kettering. New York: Paragon House, 1990, p. 11.

5. Alain Badiou mentions the following: "This examination of Plato, and singularly of the *Republic* and *Laws,* took up a good part of my 1989–1990 seminar. One day the question of the active, or non-academic usages of Plato must be deployed in all of its details. For it remains true, thereby indicating that the temporal arc of philosophy leaves us as contemporaries of the Greeks, that every philosophical decision is a decision about or from Plato."

6. See Plato, *The Republic*, V 479 d, VI 484 b, VI 486 b.

7. In Alain Badiou's words, "The void is thought of in *L'Etre et l'événement* as the suture of the situation to its being *qua* being, or as the juncture of the multiple to its own inconsistancy. It can also be said that 'void' is the name of Being. The matheme of this nomination is the theory (or deductible properties) of the empty set, such that it gives the existential launching of set theory." Cf. Méditations 4 to 6 of *L'Etre et l'événement.*

8. "These formal loans from science and art," Alain Badiou specifies, "which only concern the philosophical montage or the fiction structure of philosophy, should not be confused with the status of art and science as *conditions* of philosophy. For, in this second sense, art and science are not reservoirs of form, but loci of thinking. What they involve is not a montage caught in the resource of fiction. It is the philosophical act as an *act* of a second thought."

9. On the modalities of the subtractive, one might choose to read the final essay of this book, "Definition of Philosophy".

10. "Il ne faut plus être en désir de philosophie". Philippe Lacoue-Labarthe, *La Fiction du politique. Heidegger, l'art et la politique.* Paris: Ed. Christian Bourgois, 1987, p. 19.

11. S. Mallarmé, "Prose (pour des Esseintes)" in *Poésies.* Paris: Le Livre de poche, 1977, p. 53.

> Gloire du long désir, Idées
> Tout en moi s'exaltait de voir
> La famille des iridées
> Surgir à ce nouveau devoir.

12. S. Mallarmé, "Dice Thrown Will Never Annul Chance," in *Selected Prose and Poetry.* Trans. Mary Ann Caws. New York: New Directions, 1982, p. 127. The French text reads: "Toute pensée émet un coup de dès " and "le compte total en formation".

Definition of Philosophy

1. Alain Badiou writes: "This text is an unfolding of the definition given in the preceeding text. It was written up for the audience of my seminar, to whom I distributed it in the spring of 1991."

2. See Plato, *The Republic*, V 479 d, VI 484b, VI 486 b.

NOTES ON THE TRANSLATION

English terms appearing in the translation are in inverted commas. The original French term appears in italics. As many of the French concepts discussed here, particularly in dealing with Heidegger and Nietzsche, are translations from German, we have also included, in italics, the original German concepts when called for.

On punctuation: French authors at times tend to partake of the Proustian heritage of the long sentence. In general, I have respected Badiou's decision on length, though the semi-colon is also used. In French, it is rare to distinguish between a direct quotation and a borrowed statement, shared by a community. Both are highlighted by the use of the "accolades" (« ... »). In transcribing these to English, direct citations have been designated by the usual quotation marks, whereas expressions are given relief by use of the inverted comma.

1. Possibility

i. *La pensée* corresponds to 'thought', as does any way of characterizing thought in general, be it philosophical or scientific. But the word *pensée* when in genitive form will always appear as 'thinking', be it the thinking of history or Cantor's thinking. Whereas *une pensée*, referring to an ele-

155

ment of thought, appears as a 'thought'. The infinitive verb, occasionally made into a noun as *le penser*, particularly in readings of Parmenides, is 'thinking' as in his axiom: 'Being and Thinking are the Same'.

ii. In order to distinguish between the Heideggerian vision of history and the accounts of the science of history, we have kept the distinction established in translations of Heidegger. The French *historique* corresponds to 'historic'. Whereas *historial*, the French equivalent of *geschichtlich* becomes 'historical'. For further commentary, see John Macquarrie and Edward Robinson's translation of *Sein und Zeit*. New York: Harper and Row, 1962, p. 30, nt. 1.

iii. *La politique*. There is a major difference between politics in the activities of the State and the 'political' understood as a truth procedure or condition of philosophy, also underscored by the notion of 'inventive politics'. See below, chapter 6, "Sutures".

2. Conditions

i. The Greek sculptor, Phidias, c. 490–430 B.C., is considered to have sculpted the famed Athena statue in the Parthenon of Athens and the Zeus statue at Olympus, one of the seven wonders of the ancient world.

ii. Badiou transposes the concept of 'matheme' from Lacanian discourse, introduced in the mid-60s by Jacques-Alain Miller in "La Suture. Eléments de la logique du signifiant" in *Cahiers pour l'analyse*, n° 1. Paris: Seuil, February 1966. In Greek, *mathema* means learning. Indeed, Lacan's matheme refers to his ideal of a model endowed with the power of transmitting knowledge integrally. With Badiou, as he later goes on at length to clarify, the matheme refers to all that comes under the scientific generic procedure, or condition, of philosophy. Further remarks on Miller's concept of the matheme, and on its roots in Frege's thinking, can be found in Badiou's *Le Nombre et les nombres*. Paris: Seuil, The "Des Travaux" series, 1990, chap. 3: "Un usage contemporain de Frege", pp. 36–44.

iii. The concept of the 'compossible' stems from Leibniz who held that in God's Understanding there exists a virtual force field of logic completely unlike the space-time field. God's Understanding is said to contain a multiplicity of contradictory, mutually destructive worlds, whose possibility for co-existing is termed 'compossibility'. As with another concept that Badiou takes on, the Principle of the Indiscernibles, compossibility could not exist in actuality, hence God's choice of the "best of all possible worlds" in which Man is to live.

iv. An anecdote from the history of philosophy: the words greeting the visitor to the Academy, written on its facade.

v. The French word *événementiel* has no strict English equivalent. The usual translation of 'eventful' is *mouvementé* which refers more to what happened at a given occurrence than to the nature of the occurrence as an event. *Événementiel* refers to the phenomenon, indeed the structure of an occurrence which takes on the value of an event. The understanding of eventful should thus be steered toward the connotation of being the property of an occurrence, to which we may fix the value of a rare and exceptional nature. In sum, 'eventful' earmarks that to which we may attribute the name of an event.

3. Modernity

i. The Greek mathematician, Eudoxus, c. 380 B.C., is known to have been one of the greatest mathematicians of Antiquity. His contributions to the field are generally recognized to constitute the heart of Book Five of Euclid's *Elements*.

4. Heidegger Viewed as Commonplace

i. *retrait* is translated as 'hiddenness'. See Heidegger, *Being and Time*, p. 262, English translation [p. 219, orig. pagination]. In the original French text, Badiou employs the verb *retirer*. As the context is completely different in these cases, I have opted for "withdraw", in the sense of merely withdrawing to the sidelines of action.

ii. Existent. The term *l'étant* is the French translation of the German *Seiendes*. Macquarrie and Robinson translated *Seiendes* as 'entity'. However, due to the French use of *entité* we have opted for D.F. Krell's choice of 'existent' in his anthology of Heidegger's *Basic Writings*. New York: Harper and Row, 1977.

iii. 'Enframe'. (*arraisonnement, Ge-stell*)

iv. 'Unconcealedness'. *éclosion*. This is the French translation of *Unverdeckt*. D.F. Krell chooses 'unconcealedness' in his translation of Heidegger's "The Origin of the Work of Art", in *Basic Writings*. New York: Harper and Row, 1977, p. 174 (p. 57 of the original). We have followed suit.

v. Any translator of French philosophy will concede that terms related to language are undeniably the hardest to transfer to English. This is largely the case because the work done on this terminology in France has been rhetorical—though rarely coherent with the categories of Anglo-American philosophy of language—ever since Ferdinand de Saussure's first cast them in the *Cours de linguistique générale* (or at least since its editors cast them). While Badiou is discussing Heidegger in this passage, the debate with Lacan, who in turn translated Heidegger's important essay on language, "Logos", is ever present. Any time the notion of *le dire* is summoned, Lacan is not far behind. With this in mind, and in an effort to ease the reader's perplexity, we have attempted consistency with prior works of translation of French thought. *La Parole* is 'the Word'. *La parole de ...* is 'the voice of ....' *Une parole*, however, is quite simply 'a word'. The context should make it clear that it is not the case of *un mot*, also 'a word'. As for *le dire*, it is 'the word'. The expression 'what x is saying' also accurately translates *le dire de x*.

As for terms dealing less strictly with poetics, 'statement' translates *énoncé*, 'to utter' *prononcer* and, in the context of Jean-François Lyotard's work, 'sentence' doubles *phrase.* Once again, the reader should not expect these categories to coincide with those of the philosophy of language. (For example, P. Pecatte, the French translator of Hilary Putnam's *Philosophy of Logic* (New York: Harper and Row, 1971) casts sentence as *énoncé* or *expression* and statement as *proposition*, which does not cohere with Badiou's categories.)

5. Nihilism?

i. 'Un-binding' is a privative. When 'un' is attached to a verb, we have an opposite, for example 'untie'. Un-bound, however, derived from 'un' and 'bound', as also 'un-tie', should not be confused with the opposition of bound and unbound. Unbound: to insist on the fact that it *was* bound, though here with 'un-bound' we mean what has never been bound. In the *Categories*, Aristotle shows how those terms which fall under the heads of 'positives' and 'privatives' are not the same as ones we call 'opposites' or as he calls, 'relatives'. "To be without some faculty or to possess it is not the same as the corresponding 'privative' or 'positive'. 'Sight' is a 'positive', 'blindness' a 'privative', but 'to possess sight' is not equivalent to 'sight', 'to be blind' is not equivalent to 'blindness'. Blindness is a 'privative', to be blind is to be in a state of privation, but is not a 'privative'. Moreover, if 'blindness' were equivalent to 'being blind', both would be predicated of the same subject; but though a man is said to be blind, he is by no means said to be blindness." (*Categories*, 10, 12 a 35–41, translated by E. M. Edghill. *The Basic Works of Aristotle*, edited by Richard McKeon. New York: Random House, 1941.) It stands to reason that the possibility of thinking the un-bound requires a slackening of the will to dialectical reasoning. The intuition expressed in the following passage more significantly becomes in the *Metaphysics* the principle of the excluded middle: "that which has not yet advanced to the state when sight is natural is not said either to be blind or to see. Thus 'positives' and 'privatives' do not belong to that class of contraries which consists of those which have no intermediate.

On the other hand, they do not belong either to that class which consists of contraries which have an intermediate." (*Categories*, 10, 13 a 5–10). While Aristotle goes on to suggest that some positives may tend to become privatives, he holds the opposite as impossible. To appreciate the tension in Badiou's concept, as distinguished from any relation to prior forms of structuralism or poststructuralism, grasping the notion of the un-bound needs to be welded entirely to the irreversible condition of the privative.

6. Sutures

i. 'sexuation' or 'sexual difference'. My thanks to Professor Joan Copjec for emphasizing that Badiou is never speaking about gender.

ii. With the term of 'historical materialism', we find in the text the only usage of 'historical', a standardized one, which is not a translation of *geschichtlich* in Heidegger's sense, the term being in French *matérialisme historique* and not *matérialisme historial.*

7. The Age of Poets

i. See note 4.v.

ii. The 'real'. Although in English, the distinction between reality and the real is still awkward to place into noun form, particularly when the latter term is unaccompanied or undeveloped, philosophy has worked this concept ever since Hegel's famous dictum: "The real is rational, and the rational is real." By way of Alexandre Kojève and especially Lacan, *le réel*, in its relation to truth, has unequivocally become a stronger concept than *réalité.*

iii. *scander.* Let us recall the pre-electronic meaning of the verb 'scan': being metrically correct, admitting of rhythmic reading, cutting up into measures.

iv. 'Approach'. *accès*

v. 'bond': *lien.*

vi. the poetic statement. *le dire poétique*; see note 4.v for reference.

vii. *montage*. Badiou argues that Heidegger's 'historical' description of the forgetting of Being is as much an assembly as it is a process of editing, as with the editing of a film, with a similar degree of projection of a fictitious real. The word *montage* in French refers to the general art of editing, but it also means putting together elements in order to form a harmonious whole. We have used the term in this sense and not in the more limited way of a 'special effect', particular to the use of the concept in experimental cinema. However, the verb *monter* cannot be rendered in English as 'mount'. Its meaning is simply too restrictive. We have therefore translated the verb as 'construct', the meaning of a type of assembling being closer in this case to the French term.

viii. *Conspiration*. The need to coin this term seems to be justified by the fact that in English, any figurative meaning of two things being intricately bound cannot in any way be alluded to in 'conspiracy' without immediately having the connotations of something macabre or surreptitious going on. The source of the philosophic use of this concept is the preface of Leibniz's *New Essays on Human Understanding*, particularly where he deals with the multiple little sounds all "conspiring" together to form the overall acoustic effect of a wave.

ix. I have chosen to translate *régler* and *dérégler* by 'to order' and 'to disorder' in keeping with the Oliver Bernard translation of Rimbaud's *Une Saison en enfer, op. cit.*.

8. Events

i. The case of the privative. See 5. i.

9. Questions

i. *toute vérité est sans objet*. There is a vital pun locked into the French which must be specified. *Etre sans objet* means to be without an object, to be 'objectless'. Such is the primary result Badiou seeks in his call to disobjectivation. As he states a few lines above, "the object may well be a category of knowledge, it still hinders the post-eventful production of truths." His work to keep truth free from any association with substance or any evocation of the correspondence theory must therefor do away with the ancestral drawing board, as it were. *Etre sans objet* also means that something is no longer applicable. We shall not add anything else to the application of this predicate to truth that Badiou himself chooses not to. Let it suffice to say that when contemporary French philosophy begins to debate with the analytical tradition, the way it conceives of a philosophical object is, more than the role it attributes to logic within philosophical reasoning, at the heart of the debate— and discord.

ii. 'Unbeing'. This word, the translation of *désêtre*, formed on 'un' and 'be', is another privative, and not a reversal as in what was and ceases to be.

iii. *Adéquation. Angleichung* is the way Heidegger translates the Latin *adaequatio* and the Greek *omoima*. Adequation is usually used when translating '*adæquatio intellectus et rei*'. To highlight Heidegger's *rapprochement* between the Latin and Greek, Macquarrie and Robinson have chosen likeness, which is adopted here in translating the more Latinized French term. Cf. *Being and Time, op.cit.*, p. 257, footnote 2.

iv. Translators have differed on how to translate Lyotard's concept of *phrase*. A *phrase*, in French, is quite literally a sentence, though one need not hastily confuse the thing with its concept. But in English, a phrase is, of course, a more malleable or fragmentary entity than is a sentence. Van den Abbeele chooses 'sentence' but G. Bennington in his critical study of Lyotard prefers 'phrase', (*Lyotard: Writing the Event*, Manchester: Manchester University Press, 1988.) One should consult their respective reasons for doing so. In keeping with precedence and the text bearing Lyotard's name, we have decided to use 'sentence'.

THE (RE)TURN OF PHILOSOPHY *ITSELF*

i. 'montage'. See note 7. vii.

ii. 'fictioned'. "Après Socrate, fictionné dans la vie de sa pensée..." Badiou coins the French term *fictionné* to express someone whose existence has been re-created by way of fiction. The parallel with our neologism is complete.

iii. The *affaire Heidegger* was set off by the publication of two books: Victor Farias' *Heidegger et le nazisme* (translated into French from German and Spanish by Myriam Benarroch and Jean-Baptiste Grasset, with a preface by Christian Jambet. Paris: Verdier, 1987), which revealed new information about Heidegger's links with the German National Socialist Workers' Party, following his official resignation from the Rectorate and Party in 1934. This book, written by a former student of Heidegger's, brought into full light one of the most sensitive—and disquieting—questions confronting contemporary philosophy, questions regarding facts which, besides, all philosophers already knew about. In France, it provoked numerous responses, attacks and defenses from Heideggerians, anti-Heideggerians and critical thinkers alike (but not necessarily respectively). A text with which Badiou is here debating is Philippe Lacoue-Labrathe's *La Fiction du politique. Heidegger, l'art et la politique, op. cit.*, a sensitive response to the predicament facing philosophy as a whole, consequent to Heidegger's involvement with Nazism. Hugo Ott's *Martin Heidegger: éléments pour une biographie.* Paris: Payot, 1990, argues even more strongly that Heidegger had maintained links with the Nazi party until the end of the war.

In the interview from *Les Temps Modernes* cited in the introduction, Badiou states the following: "The argument I am defending is that in one respect all of this [i.e., the *affaire Heidegger*] is perfectly accurate, that it is entirely possible to locate in Heidegger what, at the very least, made his National-socialist involvement possible—I do not say necessary. I am also defending that this is not the center of gravity of the question, and that at least as far as the destiny of Heidegger in France is concerned—it is on this point that I am intervening more essentially—I defend that what has given *strength* to Heidegger's thinking is the very essence of the link (what I call the 'suture') he proposed between philosophy on the one hand and the poem on the other." (*op. cit.*, p. 2)

DEFINITION OF PHILOSOPHY

i. fictionings. An odd construction, indeed, but the only one apt enough to agree with Badiou's own '*fiction-nements*'.

BIBLIOGRAPHY OF THE RECENT
PHILOSOPHICAL WRITINGS
OF ALAIN BADIOU

Books

Théorie du sujet. Paris: Seuil, The "L'ordre philosophique" series, 1982.

Peut-on penser la politique?, Paris: Seuil, The "L'ordre philosophique" series, 1985.

Est-il exact que toute pensée émet un coup de dés?, Conférences du Perroquet, Paris, n° 5, janvier 1986.

L'Etre et l'événement. Paris: Seuil, The "L'ordre philosophique" series, 1988.

Manifeste pour la philosophie. Paris: Seuil, The "L'ordre philosophique" series, 1989.

Samuel Beckett: L'écriture du générique et l'amour. Paris: Conférences du Perroquet, n° 21, juin 1989.

Le Nombre et les nombres. Paris: Seuil, The "Des Travaux" series, 1990.

Rhapsodie pour le théâtre. Paris: Imprimerie Nationale, 1990.

D'un désastre obscur. (Droit, état, politique). Paris: l'Aube, 1991.

Conditions, with a preface by François Wahl. Paris: Seuil, The "L'ordre philosophique" series, 1992.

Casser en deux l'histoire du monde? Paris: Conférences du Perroquet, n° 37, December 1992.

L'éthique. Essai sur la conscience du Mal. Paris: Hatier, The "Optiques-philosophie" series, 1993.

Beckett. L'increvable désir. Paris: Hachette, 1995.

Deleuze. "La clameur de l'Etre". Paris: Hachette, The "Coup double" series, 1997.

Saint Paul. La fondation de l'universalisme. Paris: Presses universitaires de France, The "Essais du Collège international de philosophie" series, 1997.

Abrégé de métapolitique. Paris: Seuil, The "L'ordre philosophique" series, 1998.

Court traité d'ontologie transitoire. Paris: Seuil, The "L'ordre philosophique" series, 1998.

Petit manuel d'inesthétique. Paris: Seuil, The "L'ordre philosphique" series, 1998.

Essays and conferences

"Sur l'ouvrage d'Alain Badiou *L'Etre et l'événement*" (papers read by Philippe Lacoue-Labarthe, Jacques Rancière and Jean-François Lyotard, as well as A. Badiou's reply) in *Le cahier du Collège international de philosophie.* n° 8. Paris: Osiris, October 1989.

"D'un sujet enfin sans objet" in *Cahier Confrontation: Qui vient après le sujet?* n° 20. Paris: Aubier, 1989.

"Gilles Deleuze: *Le Pli. Leibniz et le baroque*," in *Annuaire philosophique.* Paris: Seuil, 1989.

"Saisissement, déssaisie, fidélité" in *Les Temps Modernes* (special edition on Jean-Paul Sartre), n° 531 à 533, vol. I, octobre-décembre 1990.

"Lacan et Platon: Le mathème est-il une idée" et "Annexes" in *Lacan avec les philosophes*. Paris: Albin Michel, The "Bibliothèque du Collège international de philosophie—rue Descartes" series, 1991.

"Mathématique et philosophie" in *Les cahiers de Paris VIII: Lieux et transformations de la philosophie*. Saint-Denis: Presses universitaires de Vincennes, 1991.

"L'outrepassement politique du philosophème de la communauté" in *Politique et modernité*. Paris: Osiris, The "Séminaire du Collège International de philosophie" series, 1992.

"L'âge des poètes," in *La Politique des poètes. Pourquoi les poètes en temps de détresse*, under the direction of J. Rancière. Paris: Albin Michel, The "Bibliothèque du Collège international de philosophie—rue Descartes" series, 1992.

"Logologie contre ontologie: Barbara Cassin, *L'effet sophistique*," in *Poésie*, n° 78, 1996.

Some interviews

"L'Entretien de Bruxelles" in *Les Temps Modernes*, May 1990, n° 526. (This interview is found in an edition of *Les Temps modernes* devoted to analysis of Badiou's system, which includes a particularly illuminating essay by Jean-Toussaint Desanti, "L'ontologie intrinsèque d'Alain Badiou".)

"L'être, l'événement et la militance," (Alain Badiou interviewed by Nicole-Edith Thévenin) in *Futur Antérieur*, n° 8. Paris: l'Harmattan, Winter 1991.

"Les réponses écrites d'Alain Badiou," in *Philosophie, philosophie*. Questions by Ata Hoodashtian, n° 4, 1992.

"Nous pouvons redéployer la philosophie" in *Le Monde*, interview by Roger Pol-Droit, 31 August 1993. Reedited in *Les Grands entretiens du Monde*, May 1994.

In English

"On a Finally Objectless Subject," translated by Bruce Fink, in *Topoi* 7 (1988), edited by Jean-Luc Nancy, Kluwer Academic Publishers.

"Descartes/Lacan" (trans. Z. Jöttkand and D. Collins), "Hegel" (trans. M. Coelen and S. Gillespie), "Psychoanalysis and Philosophy" (trans. R. Comprone and M. Coelen), "What is Love?" (trans. J. Clemens), in *Umbr(a) 1-A Journal of the Unconscious* (1996). Center for the Study of psychoanalysis and culture, Buffalo, NY.

CONTRIBUTORS

Alain Badiou was born in Rabat, Morocco in 1937. He is professor of philosophy at Université de Vincennes at Saint-Denis (University of Paris 8). He is also Conference Director at the Collège international de philosophie (Paris). As well as having written on political philosophy, aesthetics, ontology, psychoanalytic theory, logic and mathematics, Professor Badiou is also an accomplished playwright and novelist. With Barbara Cassin, he heads the "L'ordre philosophique" series at the éditions du Seuil in Paris.

Norman Madarasz was born in Montréal, Canada. He earned his B.A. at McGill University and has completed his Ph.D. in phenomenology, post-structuralism and approaches to the Anglo-French encounter at the University of Paris 8 under Alain Badiou's direction. He is former associate editor of *Philosophie, philosophie*, the journal of the Paris 8 philosophy department.

INDEX

171